The scriptural references for this book have been taken from The New King James Red Letter Ryrie Study Bible (Moody Press)

Jacket Photograph/ iStockPhoto.com, Contributor Photograph by Pete Will

Jacket Design by Cheryl McKeary

What Prompted Me to Write This Book?

How did I come upon the idea to write a daily inspirational? I don't call it a devotional for it doesn't fit the format of one. It is remarkably like a devotional however, rather than through the writer's voice, it resonates of the divine. We are indeed the treasures of our Lord's heart. He has shown me this through my writing with His direction. The title He gave me, long before I knew what I would be doing with it, was A Closer Walk. This title remained in my Bible for many months.

Years before this, a dear friend of mine sent the book God Calling to me along with some other spiritual books she had read and wanted to share. Written by two women in the 1930's and edited by a minister, the two women remained anonymous. One near suicidal, the other her close friend felt the Lord speaking to them to write. The two women compiled a book that was a year long with their daily writings, as inspired by God, within it. Those who read or have ever read it will be touched as I was, feeling as if a parent, in the spirit of our Lord, were speaking with such love and caring to you his precious cherished son or daughter. That book became a classic, translated into many languages around the world.

I kept this book close to me. I couldn't be without it through times of sadness, depression, and hardship. It spoke encouraging words to my heart uplifting my spirit and renewing my hope. At all times, I had to know this book, along with the Bible, was within my reach. Instead of reading just a daily piece, I would often read a month or two worth of writings to sooth my spirit or bring me hope for the future. Then an astounding thing happened toward the end of last year around the second week of December.

I was awakened and filled with a joy and happiness I have never felt before. It was as if the Lord had whispered in my ear that I would be writing such a book of hope. "*The time is near He told me.*" Of course, I surmised, the New Year would be beginning soon. I was being given a 'divine assignment.' I was overjoyed in the knowledge of this as I, who has always had a love of writing, knew someday I would write a book. I never imagined the type of book I would be writing. I had been published in various formats over time but, somehow writing had lost its savor to me in recent years. Now I could not contain my delight and pleasure at the thought of being chosen to write such a book. It was as if the Lord had said audibly to me " *The world is in need of a book such as this. I am giving you the assignment to write it one day at a time.* I know I couldn't get the notion out of my head that it was to be translated into many languages. This is bigger then I could ever imagine I kept reasoning to myself but it was not tedious in its inception or ever in its evolution. Instead it has been ministering to my soul throughout its entirety, often a necessary balm in this strife ridden world.

My husband, who had been sleeping beside me when all of this occurred, heard me say aloud. "Oh, this is so wonderful. I just can't believe it!" with the breathless excitement I was feeling at that moment.

"What, what are you talking about?," He inquired sleepily as I had just aroused him from a sound slumber.

This was not the time to share the moment with him so I quickly said, "Oh the New Year's about to arrive. I'm just so excited by it all!"
Boy, did that ever sound lame, even to me! Was I going to be further interrogated? I could barely contain my joy. I needed time to process this new information before sharing it with anyone.
He grumbled something about being so rudely awakened, and turned over to continue snoozing. While I, still blown away by the knowledge that I was to write such a book, lay wide awake thrilled at the prospect of what I was being asked to do.

Then, a few days before the New Year again while lying in bed awake, I was in the presence of God. My body resonated with the power of His heavenly spirit that indeed filled the room. All I could think of was how can I drop to my knees and be prostrate before Him? Since I was still lying on my back on the bed weak from sleep, never mind the vibrations my body was experiencing in the presence of our blessed Creator, I realized this would be no easy task. I could not see Him. It was dark in the room, but it was as if I were blind yet surrounded by His amazing love for me. I was paralyzed, not with fear but with a holy reverence.

I could only imagine that this being had such a sense of humor as I lay trying to figure out how I could show my respect and awe in His presence. He made it known to me that He had to tell me what I was to do, that I must stop trying to worship Him and listen.

I do not remember an audible voice but the vibrations of sound passed through my body with distinct words. This is what He said, *"You are to write this book. It will honor your bloodline and that of your pastor's family. Your grandparents were devout in their worship of Me. It will also honor the family of a dear man of God who built a church in Carmel, Maine so that others could worship as he and his family did. When without a church, they and their small congregation set about to start a new church, beginning in a large rented room. I also want to honor his extended family and their small congregation who, against all odds, built another church beginning with nothing, trusting in Me to do the rest. The new church is a testament to what true faith in Me, along with perseverance and obedience, can do. Your book will honor them as well.*

That was the message. Then He was gone.

For those reasons, I have written this book in hopes it will fulfill His purpose through me. I, as His vessel, produced this book that I was asked to write. Additional help in editing was provided by Janice Noyes, the wife of the original pastor of our church Robert Noyes, who has since gone on to be with the Lord.

When I recently reached the month of October in my writing, I was over two months ahead of schedule. I realized that He wanted this book published and soon. I thought that it was to be published before Christmas of last year as I finished it two months ahead of schedule. That was not to be, although it was made available digitally in January of this year. Instead His hand, as always, is still on this project. I'm now hoping to have it ready before Easter which would glorify our God, Jesus, His son, our risen savior and the Holy Spirit who permeates the very pages of this book.

Gloria Powell

Rejoice, for with God all things are possible. Matthew 19:26

(Written above the altar of the Carmel Full Gospel Church of Restoration, Carmel, Maine)

This Book I Dedicate to You

I am the way and the truth and the life. No one comes to the Father except through Me.

John 14:16

Just as My words of comfort bring new hope to believers. let the balm of these writings, reach the souls of My people. Such a thirst for Me has never been greater than it is today. I long to provide that oasis in the desert. Let Me reveal to you My love story for today. I desire to show all of My people My love in many languages. This book is dedicated to those who seek My face. Turn from your ways and follow Mine. This yoke, if you'll but allow it, will be easy and your burden light. When you accept Me with a heartfelt prayer, I promise that life here on this earth will be more pleasurable. It will allow you *a closer walk* beside Me, resulting in holy boldness and uncontainable joy. It is My desire to shower you with abundant blessings. Let Me pour out a new infilling of the Holy Spirit to revive you, My thirsting people. Search the pages of this, My love story to you, to know of all I have to offer. It is given freely to all but must be claimed in order to give fruit. Self reliance is taken by many as the only way to go, however, it can lead to destruction for the enemy gives it a proud face. Pride leads to arrogance which has been the devil's downfall. He desires to ensnare you as well. Follow not that path, for it leads to ruin and has sent many of My sheep astray. Also avoid indifference, rebelliousness, and self righteousness for these qualities are despised by Me. Take heed of this scripture from Matthew 22:14. *For many are called but few are chosen.* I long for you to accept My existence as your redeemer, and that of the Holy Spirit as your comforter. The Holy Spirit was My gift to all when I had to depart from the earth. So few access it. It brings such despair to Me to have My gift rejected by those who need it most. Learn more of Me. Fully accept My Holy spirit. You will never thirst again, My precious sons and daughters. I love all of you. My hope is that you acknowledge Me so I can show you the depths of this love. The pages of this book will reveal more of Me. My deepest desire is to commune daily with My people intimately, so that for now you can live a much more fulfilling life here on earth until you join Me and those you love in heaven.

Then He opened their minds so they could understand the Scriptures. Then He said to them, "*Thus it is written, and thus it was necessary for the Christ to suffer and to rise from the dead on the third day, and that repentance and remission of sins should be preached in His name to all nations, beginning at Jerusalem, and you are witnesses of these things. Behold, I send the Promise of My Father upon you; but tarry in the city of Jerusalem until you are endued with power from on high."* Luke 24:46-49

Do not leave Jerusalem, but wait for the gift my Father promised, which you have heard Me speak about. For John baptized with water, but in a few days you will be baptized with the Holy Spirit." Acts: 1-2

But the fruit of the Spirit is love, joy, peace, longsuffering, kindness,goodness, faithfulness, gentleness, and self-control." Against such there is no law. Galatians: 22, 23

January 1
Put Me First

If anyone desires to come after Me, let him deny himself, and take up his cross daily, and follow Me. Luke 9:23

When you put Me first in your life, be ready for wondrous happenings and joy uncontainable. Does that sound like such a cross to bear? It is I who did the suffering so that you can be free of the stain of sin. The blood I shed is My covering (protection) over you. Dwell in My presence daily in your quiet time. There I will be with you. Fret not of any worries then. Hand them to Me and I will clasp them to My heart. Pray, read My Word, and any other spiritual material that lines up with My Word and brings you comfort. Wait expectantly for My whisperings to quicken your spirit. Commune with Me. I will intercede for you when trouble calls. Wait expectantly. Spend time with Me. Your reward will be a closer, more intimate walk. Bask in the love I long to pour out upon you.

January 2

Learn More of Me

Blessed are the eyes that see the things you see; for I tell you that many prophets and kings have desired to see what you see, and have not seen it, and to hear what you hear, and have not heard it. Luke 10:24

The things I show to you through My Word, prayer, and obedience to My commandments will teach you more of Me. As you learn you will become like Me. It will show in all you do, desire, and say. The evil one will give you thoughts that are negative and contrary to My ways. These are easily recognizable. As I said to Satan *get thee behind Me,* you do the same. Do not entertain these thoughts for a moment for they are not of Me. You will discern My words as you grow in My teachings.

January 3

Power of Words

Know there is power in My words but also in the negative words you or others speak. Remember this, when these words positive or negative sink into your spirit, mind, and body, they influence you. Just as you do not knowingly poison your body, the temple of the Holy Spirit, with toxins for you know the difference between darkness and light. Positive words shine forth beauty, goodness, power, and righteousness. Negative words bring sadness, worry, fear, insult, hurt and guilt. They are ungodly. Dwell in divine places both in body and spirit. You will easily recognize when your mind is being tormented. I am always near, remember that. Leave no place for fear to enter. Call on My name, the name of Jesus. I will strengthen you, always.

January 4

Fear Not

Keep your mind free of fear. It is not of Me. The opposite of fear is love. I am the embodiment of love. Just desire to have this connection with Me. You will have it. I long for it. Yes, there are times when rational fear is essential. In these times ask for My guidance. I will show you the steps to take. I will grant you your desires if you but ask and if they are of My tenets. I would never wish evil or bad to come to you because a good parent only wants the best for their child. Abide in Me. Do not let fear get you in its grips. It is not of Me but of the devil. He will use it relentlessly, beware!

January 5

Smallest Details of Your Life are Important to Me.

You never know who I bring into your path for you to bless or be a blessing to you. Like the aura around a candle, the light in it spreads both inward and outward strengthens and gives hope. You won't know which ships you are bringing into safe harbors, but you are of use to Me in so many ways. You are listening when I suggest you give gifts to others either of your possessions, time, or purchases. I know of what they have need and will guide you to give the best gifts. You marvel at this but I've done it on so many occasions for you. How often have you desired an item. I would present it to you through another or direct you to the right source. Yes, even the smallest of details of your life are important to Me. As a parent desires to please, I do as well. You are deeply loved. How precious you are in My sight. I long to be cherished by you in the same way.

January 6

Rejoice in Each New Day

Another day, rejoice in it. Each new sunrise is an opportunity for change if you choose. Be it in service, character, attitude, or habits. After sleep you are revitalized. I provide for your physical as well as bodily needs. Your spiritual decisions are your choice. The Holy Spirit can and will help direct you. Trust in this, often referred to as intuition. The Holy Spirit is the conduit to your heart's desires. Remember, through all, My love never waivers. It is constant. I am here for you always. It is you who must reach or take that first step. All becomes easier after that. Put your trust in Me.

January 7

Sow Hope, Joy, Courage, and Love

Where there is despair help me sow hope. Where there is sadness help me sow joy. Where there is fear help me sow courage. Where there is hatred help me sow love.

You are My hands, My heart, My instrument. Go forth as I direct. Those words you speak may not immediately have the desired affect, but they bear fruit along the way. Even though you do not see it, I do. I bless you for it. Do not hesitate in goodness. The moments pass too quickly. Opportunities are lost. Service to Me matters more than success as this world measures it.

January 8

Ever Faithful

Be not mindful of the days passing. My time is not your time. I'll let you know if you are carrying out My plan for you. As My followers draw nearer to Me, they will be made aware of what it is I would have them do. Yes, I have a plan for all. I wish for them to fulfill it. Each of you has gifts that enable you to put that plan into motion. Know that in fulfilling it, true joy will be found. Not only will they become complete in Me, it will further My work here on earth so that I may return to gather all to Me. A shepherd is distressed if one of his sheep is lost. I am that shepherd. I fervently wish for all to return to Me from whence they originated.

January 9

Draw Near to Me

I have the supply where there is the need. Bring your requests to Me. I will honor them in My time. My stores are endless. The needs are many, especially spiritual. More and more are drawing nearer to Me. That is so comforting. To remain steady, never wavering desiring that closer intimacy can bring only joy to those, My followers, and Myself. My heart aches and soul cries out at the world events that bring such death and destruction, evidence of the evil one. He infiltrates My innocents. He blinds them to My reality. Some turn back in time. Others are lost to Me.

January 10

Press on and Worry Not

Press on. What you are doing is good. Your small acts touch others. They in turn flow on like ripples in a pond. Witness the happiness fruitful giving achieves. Your soul sings much louder in the giving then in the getting. Put these words to the test. You will know My meaning. Rest in Me always, especially when worries come upon you. Say, *I leave them with you, Lord.* Then follow through. So many have fallen into this trap of the devil. Remember this, your worry poem:

Uncrossed Bridges

Have you ever crossed a bridge
to which you never came
when a thought became a worry
a fear you could not tame?
To give precious time to worry
is an undeniable sin.

Life is a God given treasure
don't let needless worry win.

January 11

My Gifts to You

Nature is My father's best gift, after the wonder of the human body, ever changing daily. The wind, My breath, the sun, My smile, and the ocean among many other wonders of nature, are all My healing balms. Take in as much as you can daily. I give it to you freely for your enjoyment. Human technology serves many good purposes, but some can dull the senses. It can steal precious moments spent with Me or in service to others. Be mindful of your choices, some encourage progress others pull you back. Consult Me in all matters of important decisions. You will not regret this. I cannot lower the veil or reveal the plan. It would be too much for you. Pray protection daily of the whole armor of faith from helmet to sandal over all your loved ones and yourself. This is found in the Bible in Ephesians chapter 6 verses 10-18. My angels work overtime when you do, but this is good. Temptations of the world are great, many perilous. Abide in Me. I am your shield, protector, and provider. (*Elohim*).

January 12

You Represent Me

I am here when you call, doubt not. Be faithful to those I have placed you with. This is your church family. It's easy to talk of Me. Not so with others as you know, even family.
They are watching you, remember that. You are My light, representing Me and My Father.

January 13

You Too will be Persecuted

If you expect all those around you to respond favorably to your truths, visions, and writings, be forewarned. If, as you read in John 8 and 9, I who was prophesied in the Old Testament, was not welcome by many or My truths honored, how can you expect that this will be different for you? The ones who heard My voice and believed My sufferings were and are worth it, even today. You will be rewarded, dear one. Do not be weary to carry on. It is My will. I will guide you, fear not. Through you many more will be drawn to Me then you will ever know. It is My pleasure to know you are being obedient and listening to My voice in the quiet hours. I so wish others would do the same. They too would be rewarded beyond measure as you have been. Press on as I will give you the strength and holy anointing even when you think you cannot go on.

January 14

Be a Blessing to Others

Follow Me and My teachings. I set the way before you. Be mindful of what you say and do. Bless others as I have blessed you. You have it in your power to bring healings as well in My name. Do not doubt. It gives the devil a stronghold. Rest in My work. It should always be pleasurable, not tedious. Rewards will surface, both heavenly and earthly.

January 15

I am One With You

I know your pain. Each twinge, each heartache reaches the depths of My being. But I also long to bring you joy. You know this as well for I have shown you these things. As you rejoice in Me through prayer, praise, song, communion, and fellowship, our walk becomes ever deeper. Bask in it for there is more and better to come. That feeling of oneness I have with My father is there for you as well. You are beginning to experience it. As you know, it is a constant battle with the ruler of this world. His tug at the hearts, souls, spirits, and minds of My people is ever present. He takes only a small foothold in some cases to gain ground. It does take effort on your part to remain focused on Me but, the fruit you will bear will far outweigh any sacrifice on your part. Remain firm in My word and keep on in your spiritual journey. Remember, I accompany you even when you feel you are most alone. I share in your emotions and carry you when you cannot endure.

January 16

Be Expectant

Embrace each new day with expectancy. So many pleasant surprises await you. It is My pleasure to bring you happiness and spread that to others through you. You do not see the after affects but nothing is lost to Me.

January 17

Renew Your Spirit

Therefore, if anyone is in Christ, he is a new creation; old things have passed away; behold, all things have become new. 2nd Corinthians 5:17

Just as you can renew your body through exercise and correct eating, spiritually you must renew your soul as well. You found where you belong, your church family, through simple prayer: it was *Lord, you know I cannot just walk into a new church cold. Lead me to where I belong.* I sent a lost dog for you to reunite with its owner, the pastor's daughter. In answering that and many more prayers, you've since forgotten, I've led you step by step to where you are and I continue to commune. Trust in My plans for you. Others can attest to similar occasions of My heeding their petitions. Share your stories (testimonies). They strengthen your faith and bring others to Me.

January 18

Forgive as I Forgive You

Forgive those who have wronged you as I have since forgiven you. I have, long ago, forgiven My persecutors. They knew not the gravity of their offence, however, to complete My Father's plan, all had to unfold as it did. In forgiving those who have wronged you, it does not always need to be face to face. You can accomplish it in a sincere prayer or letter. There is no need to send it. The intention, in most cases is enough. However, some need face to face forgiveness to heal their own deep wounds. You will know in your spirit what to do. I will give you voice through the Holy Spirit and a peace in what you need to do

January 19

Surrounded in Love

Weary not of day to day tasks. Do them thinking to please Me. All will come easily. Rejoice in each new day. Sing, praise, pray, and adore Me as I surround you with My love.

January 20

Lean on Me to Conquer

The flesh is weak. It easily succumbs to bodily needs, but the spirit is strong. Relying on it can overcome these. Gluttony, sloth, and lack of motivation lead many to destruction. Do not bend to them, be strong. Rise on wings of eagles above those things that would defeat you. I am your constant friend and support. Lean on Me. I will help you conquer.

January 21

Be Ever Prayerful

It is so easy to become discouraged. Be of good cheer. Build yourself up constantly through fellowship, prayer, song, and teachings. I will guide you through the Holy Spirit the way you should go. I will tell you with whom you shall seek council when the need arises. But, as always, come to Me in prayer first. There you will be welcome always. I will lead you on paths of righteousness.

January 22

Seek the Mind of God

Draw closer to Me. You will feel My presence in a more real way each day. My scriptures bring life so study, read, and memorize them. They will strengthen and fortify you. It is a constant battle. You see only this world but you are being pulled and tempted continuously to fulfill the desires of the flesh. Be aware and act according to My precepts. Above all, fear not. Stay calm in Me. That will dispel confusion and torment of the mind. This is the devil's greatest tool. The mind of God should be your desire, not totally achievable but, enough to carry you through this life. Peace be with you.

January 23

Spend Time with Me, Rewards Await

Harken to My voice. When you spend quiet time with Me, limiting all distractions be it outside or in, My council to you will become more real with each encounter. This is how I am leading you. My thoughts imparted to you are always good, that is how you can discern those of Me and those of the enemy. He would have you be sad, angry, guilty, anxious, bitter, and any other negative emotion that comes to mind. These are as poison to your body, mind, and spirit. Any can become the root of sickness. This can be of the mind, especially depression, or the body, in a physical disease such as cancer. Keep evil thoughts at bay. Entertain the good by seeking Godly wisdom. Never say " I have" and fill that in with an illness because your words are powerful. You are then allowing that affliction to consume you. Your words and thought life are more powerful then you know. That is why when you are around complaining or negative people, it brings you down. The devil would have you be at their level. He delights in your misery. That quote you like so well about faith is indeed true. *When you have little faith your heart reaches out to heaven, but when you have great faith heaven reaches out to you.* (author unknown) Your spiritual experiences in a lifetime are your testimony to this. (See book preface)

January 24

Be Bold, Use My Gifts

It is so easy for your mind to experience torment over the little things said or unsaid, but imagined. Find one of My scriptures in the Bible that gives you strength. Repeat it even as a prayer. Evil thoughts must exit when met with the heavenly realm. A good one for you might be: *I can do all things through God who strengthens me.* I quoted the Bible to Satan more then once. He was forced to flee. Use the power of the Holy Spirit, the comforter, which I released upon My resurrection. Nothing else is needed but boldness, that which My apostles unleashed upon My death, to establish healings. That boldness encourages others to draw unto Me. Use it. Holy boldness is My gift to you.

January 25

Don't Hesitate to Prove Me

Like a mighty wind, the Holy Spirit can work miracles.You are its hands and feet, the bodily instrument to release its power. Doubt not. Go forth and expand your faith so I may shower you and yours with abundant blessings. I will increase your joy to overflowing. Prove Me and I will astound you.

January 26

Free Will to Choose Me

Therefore go into all the world and preach the gospel to every creature. He who believes and is baptized will be saved but he who does not believe will be condemned. Mark 16: 15, 16

My baptism is of the Holy Spirit, and joins all believers to Me. You become, in essence, the body of Christ. This unity brings power. You have become a new creature when this comes about. It puts you in opposition to those who are still seeking, yet know not what. Nothing satisfies like the relationship I fashioned to be the most natural. Yet some must suffer through a maze of wrong turns before reaching enlightenment. No need to face these harsh realities when My hand is always extended. Otherwise, if I had not given you free will, I would be instead as a tyrant demanding worship. Love Me for Me after preparing yourself. For *My yoke is easy and My burden light.* Matthew 11:30.

January 27

Proclaim My Promises

I invite all to dine at My table. It is an open invitation. The cares of this world are always present. With My nearness available in prayer and supplication I will see you through past, present, and future storms. My promises are unfailing, to be leaned upon with enduring faith. I've always held you in the palms of My hands. I will do so until I can enfold you in My arms.

January 28

Faith is Rewarded

I live in the praises of My people. The comfort felt in worship is corporate. That is why fellowship is so vital. There is a song today that states '*Better is one day in Your court than thousands elsewhere.*' You have felt this timeless joy when worshiping with others in one accord in the house of the Lord, your church. It is the sharing of My gifts of the Spirit that expands My territory. Each is given gifts suited to themselves as all have been created uniquely different. Seek the gifts I have for you. Just ask Me to show you. My plans for you far exceed your expectations. Remember with Me *all things are possible*. Look at your beautiful church which evolved from nothing just your church family's strong belief that I would, indeed, provide. It is more than any of you could ever imagine, isn't it? Your strong faith has begun to reap fruit which will bring honor to Me. This will bring favor to you and your church. Press on with love, hope, joy, and overall, patience. I always reward My faithful. I have and will fulfill all of the promises I have given you in the Bible, My Father's inspired Word.

January 29

Draw Near, God is With You

Emanuel means 'God with us.' How can you be sad, discouraged or without hope when this is My promise. Choose to draw near to Me. I will drench you with living water. Your joy is My desire always. Bask in My love. This too will come.

January 30

Your Purpose I will Reveal

I marvel in you and the great things I've set forth for you to do. Be still, listen, and wait. You will not be disappointed. Walk beside Me. We can move mountains!

January 31

Intimacy with Me Brings Peace

In all you do seek to please Me. In all accomplishments be joyous. Each day a new beginning to touch others, encourage, uplift, and show love. My wisdom is yours whenever needed. Seek it in simple prayer. There is an endless supply. No need to fear or to be anxious for anything. Your intimacy with Me will bring a peace, a tranquility you have often found in nature. Doubt not, you are loved, cherished, and held dear. You are a unique creation with gifts untested. They are awaiting to be unwrapped. My provisions are boundless. Test Me. You will see My ever faithful one.

February 1

Go forth in My Strength

I give you strength when you need it. Lean on Me always. How can I prove Myself if you aren't ready to ask for help? I can lighten your burden, try Me. Go forth today in My strength not on your own. Look to the beauties around you. For you I proclaim My gifts. Your eyes perceive them and, yes, I provide them. The sparkle of the ice lit snow, the expressions on a newborn's face, the star studded skies and foam crested waves are all for you, My beloved.

February 2

The Sweet Incense of Worship

The sweet incense of your love drifts upward. It is pleasing to Me. I am so delighted with your worship, especially when in fellowship with others. I will help you find your way. I understand your hardships. Through them you always grow. I see it, though you do not.

February 3

Your Attitude is Your Choice

A positive attitude will get you so much further then a negative one. Your spirit projects emotions unknown to you. Others can detect impatience, indifference, and so many other emotions just as you can sense them in others. Choose to be happy, joyous, and upbeat, rather than carrying around those negative emotions which are like chains weighing you down. They are such a drain physically, more then you can imagine. You are My unique creation offering your own personality, talents, and opinions. No one is better or less then you. Treat all the same. That is My way. So much sadness, despair, poverty, unkindness, and brutality have transpired due to unfair treatment to others by those in higher positions or who somehow feel superior. All could have been so easily avoided. I see and chastise in My own way those who deserve it. It is so much more pleasurable to be gracious, bestowing unexpected gifts both of the material world and the spoken word. To uplift, that is the goal which travels far beyond the one who has been blessed.

February 4

The Gift of Life

Each day is a gift from Me to cherish and guard as gold. How many in prisoners long to be where you are and experience your freedoms for just one day? Exalt in the wondrous body God has given you, capable of so many processes going on without your care or knowledge. Birth is a joyous miracle. Life is My precious gift to you. Cherish it. Do not complain. Praise Me even in the tough times. I will pull you through and mold you more into My image.

February 5

I Will Carry You Through the Fire

Love all you meet. Give a smile even to strangers. For some it is the only kindness they may have experienced in a long time. So many smile whose hearts are breaking. Their outside demeanor often hides their core. Be charitable, loving, kind, and a listening ear, as needed. You have been there. Be ready to give back what you have received. I come to those who call out to Me in affliction. I can sooth the weary soul. You can attest to this. Long suffering can be like the refining process of precious metals bringing beauty to the surface. Press on. I will carry you through the fire.

February 6

Doubt Not

Bury doubt, the greatest tool of the deceiver. Wisdom, hope, faith, truth, love, kindness, patience, joy, and grace shall abide in you through Me. I give you the tools with the Holy Spirit. Claim them. My power is yours, so accessible. Just ask, accept, and use.

February 7

I am Your Spiritual Anchor

Deny Me and you let go of your heavenly anchor. You become tethered to the earth and its values. Eternity awaits. Earthly life is temporary. Seek My face, My approval in all you do. My wisdom and guidance will reveal itself in your work, your dealings with others, and your spiritual life. Yes, as you draw closer to Me, you will be richly served but, your service will also be required. Fear not, for you will be blessed for it.

February 8

The Divine Spark

I hear your prayers, the desires of your heart. Face each new day with renewed determination. Pray that My will be done. I will uncover all you need to lead a more fulfilling life. Even those most close to you will be drawn closer to Me through you. My light will shine upon you. Don't hesitate to prove Me. Draw strength and power through Me and My ever present Holy Spirit. It is the earth magnet to Me which I have given to all of My creation. The key is to recognize, accept, believe, and live in the hope of its power in you. It is for all but so few harness its energy. Instead they become slaves to the flesh seeking only earthly pleasures. Such a waste of the divine spark I have placed within all, easily activated through faith. Their candles (inward spiritual glow) could burn so ever more brightly but instead they choose to extinguish them in gluttony, lies, drink, immoral living, or some other debauchery so foreign to their inherent spiritual nature, My intended dwelling place. I cannot inhabit an environment of darkness. I embody light, truth, love and goodness, My precious child search no longer and seek My face. In Me you will be fulfilled. Forsake the treachery of the devil who wishes your destruction.

February 9

Faithfulness Rewarded

Your faithfulness will be rewarded. I see your loneliness, pain and daily struggles. I am guiding, unseen, upholding, and helping you shoulder your burdens. Your strength comes through Me. There is much to spare. Beware of feelings of guilt, remorse, sadness, worry, and fear. These sap your strength. They are not of Me. At the first signs of these proclaim *Jesus is my rock, my deliverer, and my provider. To Him I give these thoughts to banish them from my being. Joy and peace replace them now in Jesus name, Amen.*

February 10

Holy Boldness

Boldness is foreign to your nature but vital to bring new life to your spirit. Embrace it. Picture holy boldness and the power of it. I give it freely for your pleasure. Claim it, another of My promises. Through the Holy Spirit, it is yours. Experience the peace it brings. You will not regret it or be disappointed. For it is this new life I desire for you. It will satisfy your every need. Do not forsake the gift of the Holy Spirit. I won't have you, My dear one, regret your decision later on. My wisdom and truth verifies its validity and that it is the fulfillment of My promise of a comforter for My dear ones when I had to leave their earthly realm.

February 11

A Daily Prayer

Accept each new day as a fresh adventure. Avoid a mindset that predicts what will befall you. Often when you do, it can prove to be unpleasant. Get up and say *I will let You direct my day, my attitude, and my mindset.* I long to bless you. I will in unexpected ways. My wisdom will guide you in all you do if you allow Me to help you by seeking Me in prayer, even for the simplest of decisions. Pray *Dear Lord guide me in this day to be a light unto You and* a *blessing to others in unexpected ways. Let me experience the joy you have for me as you have promised in Your Word for Your believers.* I will honor this prayer. I will show you all I have for you. Be expectant, wait patiently but with faith. I will be there for you.

February 12

Praise Me

My grace is sufficient for all your trials. Worry not, your needs will be fulfilled. It is when you doubt that allows negativity to enter your life. Fear is a part of that as well as guilt, uncertainty, and negative thoughts. I long for your happiness in this world and in the world to come. You are precious to Me. I will show you how each new day in many different and unexpected ways. Look at all there is to be thankful for. Your complaints will seem unnecessary. They, like the murmurings of the Israelites in their quest for the promised land, hinder joy and keep away the good things I have for you. Praise, when you are feeling down. You will be uplifted in spirit, I promise you.

February 13

Cultivate a Cheerful Attitude

I bring you fresh living water daily through the Holy Spirit. Drink of it. It is there to enliven and uplift you. Read My Word, pray, and spend quiet time with Me. I will be there for you. Like a refreshing night's sleep, you have this resource always available. Cultivate a cheerful attitude. With practice it will become natural. I would that you could live in paradise with Me, but until that time, plant your earthly garden with love, joy, peace, tranquility, and hope. My resurrection should bring all to Me in thankfulness and anticipation. Draw near to Me daily. You will know I am with you.

February 14

You are Loved

If you never experience love again, you can be assured that My love for you will endure for eternity. So many have been hurt by a trusted person. Through that pain they choose to never give love another chance. They are foolhardy for, love is My greatest gift . There is someone out there whom I have chosen for you. Seek with untiring faith. Believe that I will provide. I will indeed. The secret of true love is the give and take of it. You must be willing to sacrifice just as your partner must. You take care of each other. I take care of you both. Don't let self absorption ruin a good thing. Some are destined to be alone, but they are never truly alone. I am with them always. Seek My protection. I will provide it.

February 15

Heed My Words

Heed these words I impart. They are for you in hard times. I would not help you to form them if I didn't care about you and others who will read them. It is too easy, as you so recently have seen, to become discouraged, disillusioned, and down hearted. You must draw strength from Me or things will only get worse. It is true the enemy attacks the devout. He does it in such sly ways that can tear you away from My teachings. Beware of this. Fight it with all you have for it is only those that stay the course who can gain My kingdom both here and in eternity. I bring encouraging words to draw you and others closer to Me. Doesn't that upset the enemy! Why do you think the struggle has been so hard. All the forces of evil are directed toward you at this time. To fight this evil you must put on the full armor of faith daily, read My Word, and pray for protection. (See Ephesians 6: 10-17) The world knows not of the spirit realm or of the powers that battle unseen for the souls of My dear ones. Do as I direct. Put your trust in Me once again. I will carry you when the need arises.

February 16

Look to Me Not to Others

Be unmindful of earth's time. For this go by My timetable, that is, trust your heart to direct you in all you do. Consult with Me if you are unsure. Guard against your flesh to make decisions for you, especially regarding your all important assignment. My plans for you have been there for many years. I have been preparing you for this endeavor. Never doubt that you are now fulfilling My wishes. Look not to others. That is where you will allow confusion to enter. This has been the cause of your discouragement with this mission. I will and have directed you. I will continue if you remain faithful to Me.

February 17

My Hugs and Kisses

The pets I allow are My hugs and kisses, My gifts to you along with sunsets, starlit nights, warm breezes, children's giggles, and so much more. Cherish these at their unexpected arrival as they are some of My ways of showing My delight in you. Look for the good in all. Different does not mean inferior, just a unique personality. Learn to deal with them on their terms not yours. You will find things go easier for you. You can learn from others as they can from you, even the children. They are so fun loving. You must understand them to reach them. You have discovered how to do this. Let their sense of wonder overflow to you, that which is so evident in children and pets. They will be drawn to you as never before. It is better not to force your ways upon them for it will just push them further from you. Let them direct, you follow, and the naturalness of it will evolve. Keep it playful. Then it becomes learning with a fun twist. Let them guide you and, as you follow be creative in your play, it can be a great learning tool. Then it becomes fun for the child and you as instructor. That is why they are drawn to you. Be not discouraged with what you see with earthly eyes. I've created them perfectly. You can help to bring out that perfection. Seek My guidance. I will not disappoint you. Your happiness is My desire. I will fulfill your wishes if you will just trust in Me.

February 18

Refresh Your Spirit, Worship

*The thief cometh not, but for to steal, and to kill, and to destroy: I am come that they might have life, and that they might have it more abundantly***.** John 10:1

I long to revive My saints in their struggles. The world daily weights them down. I came to give life and more abundantly. Reach out for your due in joyful acceptance. I will revive those old dry bones and bring rivers of living water throughout all of their tissues and sinews. That is why I allow others to pray for you and intercede through the Holy Spirit in groaning and heartfelt pleadings. My plan was always for a church body to represent Me and work toward my goals of bringing others to Me through salvation, teachings, and prayer. The church mentioned in the preface of this book is such a church. But the law, as in the days of old, can take the place of righteousness, mercy, love, and kindness. It is still fair to say that *love thy neighbor as thyself* sums up the kind of empathy we must have for one another. Oh, that religion had not gotten for itself such a bad name as the strength in group worship cannot be underestimated. We all can care for each other, not just in our immediate families, but with our work associates, other social networks, but especially our church families. You, who are imperfect, can be made more perfect in My likeness when gathered in an assembly with spirits in one accord of joyful and reverent worship. Religious dogma can and has ruined a good thing. It must be guarded against. Seek My face in all regards. I will lead you in My perfect ways. You miss such a glorious experience of unity and love when you do not access your church family, a divine extension of you earthly family.

February 19

God Centered

Look not to others, but to Me to guide you. I will direct you to a God centered church and to likeminded worshipers where you will be refreshed, refilled, and rejuvenated. Do not allow worry, doubt and confusion to enter your mind for, I will help you with that if you but ask. My goal is to draw others to Me through you and fellow worshipers. The world is a desperate, lonely place where the discontent of humanity cannot be filled with earthly things. Money, power, possessions, even fame, all lose their draw once tasted and achieved. The hungry heart searches to fill its spiritual needs in all the wrong places bringing defeat, depression, illness, and often addictions. These can be food, drugs, alcohol, pornography, illicit sex, and other less common ones such as television, computer games and hoarding to name a few. Become God centered. Through this relationship, all you need will be supplied. You will never hunger or thirst for earthly things in the same way again.

February 20

Perfect Love

I view My creation with a perfect love. Oh, that you would acknowledge Me. If only you would realize all that I have for you is at your command, as close as your fingertips. Such an abundant love I long to pour out to you, if you spend time with Me in prayer, My Word is one place you'll find Me. Also in a solid Bible believing church that allows My Holy Spirit to minister naturally to those in need. Look about you. Places of worship are everywhere. Choose and let your heart and spirit guide you to where you belong. Open this exquisitely wrapped package I have for you. You will not be disappointed. The time is short and the workers are few. You are called to represent Me to a despairing, hurting world. Harken to My call before it is too late. Remember there is strength in numbers. Fellowship with others of like mind in joyful worship. This way your spirit will be continually renewed. It is My way of recharging your batteries. Be bold, enter in, taste, and see for yourself. You will be delighted at how wonderful you feel. Your whole view of this life will be altered for the good. Then it will be as if you cannot get enough of this living water. Time, as seen in earthly ways, is suspended. The delight experienced in such heartfelt worship cannot be overemphasized. Taste and see. I promise, you will not be disappointed. I give it freely for you to reach out and take. Don't miss it by being inhibited, stubborn, or narrow minded. The comforter, in the person of the Holy Spirit, is Who I left when I departed. When you ignore My gift, it is an insult. The same way you would feel if you gave Me a wonderful gift and I never acknowledged it. Seek a spirit filled church with like minded people. You will be fed as I intended. You will also soon see revival as never before. As I have constantly said *I long to bless My people*. So many have and will turn away. For those who hunger and thirst, accept My living water.

February 21

Children Reflect My Purity

If you but knew the love I have for you. My faithful presence hungers with a desire for a relationship with you. If you were aware of it, your feet would run to Me without thought of why or what others would say. You would fulfill your heavenly calling. You would be drawn ever closer becoming more like Me naturally, the ultimate desire of your spirit man. If you could see through spiritual eyes all would become clear. The earth and its precepts have caused your eyes to become as covered with a film or veil. Why do you think children are so precious? They have recently been close to Me, yes, in My presence. They radiate My beauty in their innocence and purity. That is why they make you laugh at their antics.

February 22

Unearthly Fragrance

Have you ever enjoyed the fragrance following a rain storm? It is the most pure, divine scent. Anyone who has ever experienced it will remember it fondly. Think of Me, Jesus, as this is as close on earth as you can come to Me in the realm of the senses. Yes, next to that can be said, the sweet smell of an infant whose spirit has recently been with Me. Here is the embodiment of fresh, sweet, untarnished beauty. This is only one of the senses that you will experience in heaven. Can you but imagine all the others along with the precious presence of your heavenly Father? He will heap blessings upon you as you soak up the glory you will behold there. The waiting is worth it. Just picture the beauty, joy, and fulfillment. If you look forward to that, you can endure the hardships you face in this life. Carry this hope with you. It will sustain you through the hard times and lighten your burdens.

February 23

Rejoice in All You Have

I have given you untold blessings. Think not of what you lack but, dwell on what you possess. Nothing is yours in the end. You have no need of earthly things then. Your reward will far exceed anything you can imagine. Hang on to that hope. You will inherit My kingdom, My Father's house. Remember My promise: *Eye has not seen, nor ear heard, nor have entered into the heart of man the things which God has prepared for those who love Him.* 1st Corinthians 2: 9.

February 24

My Love is a Covering Over You

I came to bring life and more abundantly. My brief time on earth, as one of you, gave Me insight into your struggles, heartaches, and the torment you must deal with, sometimes daily. That is why I have given you My father's gift of the Holy Spirit to guide you when you cannot see clear of the obstacles before you. Spend time in prayer, seek guidance through Him (the Holy Spirit), and you will be given the words you need at your time of need. Effortless should be the moment when you are tried, for I have promised *I will be with you and never leave you.* If you grasped this, your burdens would be so much lighter. Go in peace with this assurance of My presence. Rejoice in the ever protecting love I have for you.

February 25

Live Fully

My love should be sufficient. Look not to the world for guidance. Man doesn't have the wisdom and answers unless I provide them or send others, in human or angelic form, to speak for Me. Welcome all who come into your life as they are all there for a reason and, even though it often is not evident, I bring them to receive what you have for them or to teach you in ways you could not learn on your own. What you need to know I am revealing to you daily in ways sometimes least expected. Even you can see the humor in the mundane happenings that seem routine but are not. Enjoy this life in a way you never have before. Look not to it as work but as a sacrifice to Me. The reward may be money but much more awaits you on the other side. Live fully in each moment. I mean for it all to be pleasurable. Picture Me as a loving Father, smiling down on you with loving thoughts. Say "*Abba (father) look what I am doing. I hope you are well pleased as I do it out of love for you."* My purpose is to shower you, who have loved Me, with blessings to exceed anything you could envision. Wait upon Me and you shall see. I smile upon you when you seek to please Me.

February 26

Pray Unceasingly

Pray unceasingly. That sounds difficult, but prayer can become more a part of your everyday life without being a hardship. Think of it as a conversation with me. In all things look to Me as in how to order your day, and to whom you are to relate. Some days are organized by set labor, however, others leave you free to have more choices. Try to be a blessing with a note, a visit, a phone call, an email or just a small gift. You will reap the benefits more then the person you are blessing. Be of service to others. You will receive a double blessing, as both you and the recipient are blessed. The cheer you bring the downhearted will bless you threefold. Be an encouragement by speaking words of hope and love. Share My love. Be a light unto a world fraught with darkness. Your goodness will give you victory over negativity in others by speaking My truths.

February 27

Grow in Me

Wisdom does not come easily. Growth spiritually is also a gradual process. The knowledge I have for you comes when you are mature enough to handle it. That is why I can't reveal more than you can bear. Your questions I answer as you ask them through others, My Word, or the Holy Spirit. Strive to continue to grow in Me. Active worship brings others closer to you. You become closer to them in a holy union. Never cease to pray for others as they have prayed for you. These are ways that you can continually renew your spirit and theirs as well. When I bring someone to mind, it often is for you to pray for a need they have. Give them a call, send a letter or email but be an encouragement. You needn't know what the need is. The Holy Spirit does and can intercede for you to provide what is lacking. I will reveal later what has transpired. You will be allowed the knowledge of what your prayer has accomplished through Me.

February 28

My Angels Watch Over You

I have taken you through many storms, not of your making, both of nature and in the physical. At these times My angels have watched over you, given you protection, and brought you to a safe place. The prayers of others have covered you with My protection as well. I have heard your cries to Me. That is when I've been closest to you. You have not always felt My presence. But more often you have. It has brought you comfort. Make time for Me in your busy day. I will calm your spirit and guide your ways throughout the day. Remain at peace in all circumstances. I will provide the grace to make the right choices.

February 29

Mighty Warriors for Me

In this changing world, be ready to alter your course as needed. Have your armor ready as Satan will try to meet you at every turn, especially when you are in unfamiliar territory. That is when you are at your weakest. Look to Me for your protection, cling to those powerful Bible verses such as *Greater is He that is in me, than he that is in the world.*(1st John 4:4) Boldly claim the name of Jesus and, with a mighty "alleluia," go forth with the confidence of victory. Legions of angels will be round about you to protect you and intercede in battle. Fortified with the full armor of God, you are battle ready. Go forth with My banner over you, as mighty warriors for Me.

March 1

Be Ready for the Unexpected

Your day is not always as you planned. Even in this I am a part. As I have already said, be ready for the unexpected and to be blessed by it. Proceed with courage and holy confidence. I will provide the knowledge needed. You are already beginning to see this. It will only get better. Trust in Me. Others are being touched by your kindnesses. They are being drawn closer to Me through you. They are not aware, but this is so. I tell you these things to build up your faith.

March 2

Spiritual Exercise

Your faith needs spiritual exercise which is prayer, just as your body needs exercise to maintain and increase strength. Do not neglect any aspect of the mind, body, or spirit.. Like the trinity, God, Jesus, and the Holy Spirit, all need to be worked on in your daily life to expand your growth. Continue praying for the protection of your loved ones. Try to remember to do this daily. These prayers make a difference. They are working in other ways to draw those nearer to Me. I and my angels are busy long after you are finished praying, ministering to those you care about. They are beginning to feel My presence. They are being comforted and I, as well, in the knowledge that you are being obedient and that

My own are returning to Me. I hope to bring you peace in these words and a renewed spirit today and always, My dear one.

March 3

Maintain Calmness

I have made it easier for you, when you thought it would be difficult. Maintain the calmness I've instilled in you. You can accomplish so much more. Worry expends energy better used to be creative in your daily activities whether work or leisure. Slow your step, inhale the fresh air, glory in the warmth and radiance of the sun. I give these to rejuvenate you. Don't plan too far ahead. Each day know your limitations and stop when you are beginning to feel depleted. If you go beyond you will regret it in attitude, energy, and health. Your calmness and confidence will give those around you more of these qualities to uplift them as well. They will see Me in you but in a subtle way. Goodness and kindness begets these qualities and draws others closer to Me indirectly. These seeds, you are unconsciously planting, will yield the fruit I desire. Continue, as you have. I will renew your energy and zeal for life as never before. Love those you encounter as you love yourself. All will be well where ever you go. The peace that passes all understanding is My promise and gift to you. Accept it as My blessing in this sometimes hectic world.

March 4

Commune With Me

Already you are beginning to reap the benefits of being faithful to Me. If you have been reading My words and being obedient, you are being rewarded. The surprises I reveal at unforeseen moments will both excite you and increase your faith. You are beginning to see examples of this happening almost instantaneously which has surprised you most of all. I long to shower My loved ones with blessings daily. When they heed My words and seek Me in prayer I can commune with them. This is a dual blessing for both of us. I treasure this time with you. Try not to neglect it as it is beneficial and brings spiritual growth.

March 5

Irresistible Presence

Others are being drawn to you more naturally now as you draw closer to Me. It is inevitable as My spirit in you is as a magnetic force. It is irresistible for I am at one with My Father's children. This God force cannot be ignored. You are dear to Me .Those who seek to find Me, are drawn to those who have Me. Continue to be faithful and devoted in all you do. Your belief, obedience, and prayers will continue to draw others to you and thus to Me. Radiance attracts others. This love light, as the sun, is both a warming and comforting presence and quite irresistible.

March 6

Renewed Energy

I inhabit the praises of My people hence, when you are with a group who are in one accord, those present experience the comforting anointing of the Holy Spirit. As you dwell in this, it draws you closer to Me and I to you. Such loving communion with My precious children gives Me great pleasure and you newfound joy. Seek this whenever possible as it rejuvenates your spirit, as a battery is recharged, giving you renewed energy, resilience, and stamina to face the trials ahead. Drink it in and get your fill. I offer it gladly and freely. Picture Me smiling down upon you as it is true. Tell others to observe the multitude of churches. They must locate one where they can feel My presence as you have. They will never regret it once they find where their heart, mind, and soul can be fed.

March 7

Be Not Afraid.

Dispel that feeling you get in your spirit when you listen to negative thoughts concerning your fears. Your sadness, anxiety, bitterness, and resentment can all produce a heaviness there almost making you physically sick. It's that sinking feeling you all experience at times when you've said the wrong thing or done something you are not proud of. This area is located in your center or physically the middle of your diaphragm just above your navel. Notice and correct immediately by not accepting it. Then carry on and I will help you accomplish that which you fear. Fill that space with lightness of spirit, joy, gladness, enthusiasm, and warm feelings toward others. Now doesn't that feel better?

March 8

Do Not Dwell on Lack

Enjoy what I've provided. Do not dwell on lack but rather all that you have been given. I have and always will provide for your needs, worry not. You are bombarded with earth's values, daily attempts to convince you that fulfillment will come with a purchase of this or that. Fulfillment, true fulfillment, can be found in Me alone. If in doubt seek My face, through prayer, teachings, fellowship, and the earnest desire to draw closer to Me. I promise that you will not be disappointed. Draw nearer, time is short.

March 9

Nourish Your Spirit

Just as the body cannot function properly when one of its parts is injured, neither can the spirit without its proper nourishment. Desire to learn more of Me and your spirit will be fed. Seek like believers and your growth will be accelerated. Ask for discernment so that you can know if your teachings and associations with others are of God. You are all given gifts of the spirit that compliment each other when you are gathered with My followers. You will see these gifts come to fruition in the latter days. Just as each part of your physical body has its purpose, these gifts used together in your worship and life can accomplish much. I am working through all to bring unity, purpose, and a new sense of power and boldness needed to further My kingdom.

March 10

Ask Me

As I draw your loved ones nearer, you will see they are observing and listening to you more. Don't think you can't learn from them. It's a back and forth process. For example, think of prayer and its purpose. It has been summed up so well by the acronym ACTS. The reasons for prayer are **a**doration, **c**onfession, **t**hanksgiving and **s**upplication. Easy to remember, right? There's more if you try to figure it out. These letters fall precisely in their order of importance. Adoration pleases Me most, yet simple gratefulness for all you've been given and who I am is often the last thought of why you should pray. Confession is of a contrite humble heart. It reaches inward to a man's soul touching Me deeply. I and the angels rejoice when this happens. Thankfulness, yes third in order, is also welcome anytime. It uplifts us both. Lastly, but often first in so many prayers, is that of supplication or asking. I do not hesitate to answer prayers, but I may do it in My time not yours. If My followers were more educated in the effectiveness of prayer they would pray unceasingly as I have suggested in My word. Remember when you were trying to remember what the 't' meant in the acronym ACTS? I understood the frustration you felt at not remembering it. Then you thought you could wait and ask someone else. "Why not Me," I asked? You did and were astonished at how instantaneously I replied, "*thanksgiving*." If only you and others would come to Me first before turning to someone else in matters both large and small. I await, ready to bless, try Me.

March 11

My Plans for Your Life

All should be excited about the truth and promise that I have a plan for the lives of My creation and that, when you draw near enough to Me to begin to hear My voice, I slowly reveal it to you. Then I order the steps you are to take to fulfill it. Your spirit will leap within you as I in Mary's womb when she met with her cousin Elizabeth to proclaim My eminent birth. You have felt this recently and know the joy of it. (See book preface) The happiness you feel affirms that you are fulfilling My plan for you. It is like a birthing process as you are beginning to find out, but the blessings that will come from it will further My kingdom and bless you abundantly. You are beginning to see these blessings.

March 12

The Pieces all Fit

As you look back on your life you will see how it is like a puzzle to which I have given you small pieces. As you have grown, the pieces began fitting together and making sense. Just as you now may be living in the location of your heart's desire, your mate as well, was sent to fulfill your wish for true love. This you so deserve after an earlier life of suffering and hardship with a self centered uncaring spouse. The irony is that you are the perfect match for him as well. He has been telling you this repeatedly lately. Is this not so? Yes, as with you, I have the perfect plans for those who are faithful to Me. This does become apparent as My followers draw closer to Me. All that is required is obedience, love, faith, prayer, and fellowship with others of like mind. Leave the rest to Me. I will continue to order your steps, guiding you onward to righteousness, in your life's journey.

March 13

My Plans for Your Life

You are continually realizing that I have been faithful to you in so many ways. Yes, I know the desires of your heart. I hasten to fulfill them. You are living where you wish from a simple heartfelt prayer that I granted without your realizing it until now. I brought the right people to you to grant this prayer. Even down to the smallest details did I give you your heart's desire. Never doubt My love and care for you which will continue now and forever. You are dear to Me. I am well pleased with what you are doing. As you share your testimonies of My working through you, not only is your faith expanded but you are teaching others of My ways. This is drawing them closer to Me. As a shepherd, I cannot bear to lose any of My flock.

March 14

Tap into My Power

For the message of the cross is foolishness to those who are perishing but to us who are being saved it is the power of God. 1st Corinthians 1:18

When tapped this power can produce good works, miracles, healings, hope for the hopeless, and bring joy to the downhearted. Seek to be used of Me. I will demonstrate what can be accomplished.

March 15

Rest in Me

Enjoy all that I am providing. I have so much more. A time to rest the spirit and be rejuvenated does good for the soul. Don't hesitate to stop to look around you and enjoy the view, interact socially, or savor a pleasant meal. You give so much in your daily life, allow Me to pamper you for this short time. I see your pleasure. I long to bless you more. Accept, be grateful, and be good to yourself. Don't hesitate to stop and listen for My voice without any distractions to interfere. Do this daily. It will rest your harried mind while making a Godly connection. It is in these times I am able to commune with you. Don't neglect these precious moments. They will increase your happiness and I delight in your joy.

March 16

Be Patient

I am revealing more of Myself daily to you. Take it in. Marvel at it. There is more as I have promised. It only gets better. Yes, the smaller frustrations of this life will always be there. Even they have a purpose. Sometimes just to teach you to have more patience.

March 17

Rejoice in My Plans for You

Seek the quiet times and My voice. It is then that I speak to your heart. I know your desires and, when you are patient, I gradually unfold My plans for you. Do not despair. You will know assuredly what I have for you to do. I give the strength, energy, and Holy Spirit to help you carry out the life I have mapped out for you. You will know as the joy and peace that passes all understanding will bubble up inside of you as a confirmation. Wait expectantly. Some already know and have had this experience. Long and pray for it. I will be faithful. It is one of My many promises for those who diligently seek Me.

March 18

My Gentle Spirit

I promised to be with you always. That means when you need Me most. The trials that are ahead will be made lighter by My gentle presence. When occasion has you to worry think of Me carrying you and yours through the fires and flood waters. Be calm and still. You will feel My presence. The peace that passes all understanding is yours. Put a song in your heart. Let My joy fill you with the pleasure I desire for you and those you love. Enjoy your time together as a special family reunion and bask in the love I desire for every family. You are all very special to Me. I long to bless everyone abundantly and turn sadness into joy. That is My specialty. Drink of the living water I'll pour out to your spirit and the renewed energy it brings to your physical body.

March 19

Each Day a New Surprise

I even surprise you with the weather, never predictable. Don't complain, instead look for the beauty all around you. You will easily find it. No day is ever the same. Be grateful for that for some days do try your nerves. They are also to build up your patience and to increase your thankfulness for all that you do have. Try to notice something new each day. Stop to enjoy the beauty before you in nature and the company you keep. Even the birds sing for your pleasure. Imagine Me singing to you and you will come close to the truth.

March 20

The Church, My Spiritual Body

How your life has changed in these short weeks. You have been obedient and are listening to My voice in your quiet times in nature, prayer, and even the songs you are choosing to listen to. Have I not blessed you in unexpected ways as I promised? You don't realize what a blessing you are to others as the joy you radiate can only go forth like a beam of light. These blessings I have for all if only they would heed My voice, be obedient, and fellowship with others who love Me in like manner. As the human body is made up of many parts, the spiritual body can be likened to it. When a group gathers in My name, they are given special gifts through the Holy Spirit, unique as are their personalities. These gifts, working together, bring unity of purpose. They are available to build faith, draw others to Me, and renew hope in all who are exposed to them. They are given freely by Me, through My father, and need only to be desired. Yes, you have tasted of these and, through being drawn closer, are experiencing renewal in your physical and spiritual walk. Do not deny these gifts for, in so doing, you are neglecting the nourishment of your soul. I wish to bestow them upon you, if you but ask, to draw you nearer to Me. You will never regret moving forward in this manner. I long to pour out My love to you. Accept this free gift for it will bless you as much as Me.

March 21

Importance of Prayer

Pray for others as they come before you in thought. You have been prayed for. With prayer has come protection. Never underestimate the power of a heartfelt prayer. It is another freedom, seldom used by many to further their cause. If answered prayer were kept track of by those who actively fervently pray, the supplicants would be amazed by how many are granted. It is My pleasure to give you that which you need to feel complete here on earth. I desire to make your journey a pleasing one. If all would pray as I instruct in adoration, confession, thanksgiving, and supplication, life would be made easier. Action brings rewards. Your kind gestures bless you and others. Do not neglect to pray.

March 22

Bind Fear, Cultivate Confidence

You have followed My teachings about not allowing fear to enter your life in thoughts. By stopping it at first appearance, you have not been attacked by the evil one. Do not leave a door open to fear. Do not even entertain it for a minute. The anxiety it can bring can only do harm physically, mentally, and spiritually. Bind fear before it has a chance to find a place. Say this simple prayer, *Lord replace any thoughts of fear with love and kind feelings.* Your life will take on a new radiance, evident to others. They will gravitate toward you as the confidence you exude is like a wave causing others to feel its power. They will desire what you have. I never intended for those of this world to feel any other emotions then joy, gratitude, love, humility, and serenity. All you need I can provide and do so willingly.

March 23

Life's Challenges Have Prepared You

You are stepping out boldly as I advised and bringing such comfort. Thank you for being obedient. I do not put these thoughts in your spirit to be ignored, but to be acted upon. As you become more sensitive and discerning you will acknowledge the needs of others more intuitively. Listen to My voice. You will know what to do and pray. Your tender heart and the challenges you have met in life, have prepared you for My service.

March 24

You are Never Alone

Know and be strengthened that I am with you through it all as My father was with Me in My journey to earth. What I faced no human should ever endure. The plan and its purpose was fulfilled so that all could experience God's glory, mercy, and forgiveness. All of man's good works could never make up for sin. My sacrifice was worth it to free all spirits from its stain. Be grateful daily for the gift of life and the beauty around you. It is shorter then you think no matter how many years you live. Fill each day with the best of yourself. I am your constant help. Look to Me when difficulties arise. I will guide you to victory.

March 25

Stop Fear Before it Takes Hold

Hold fast to My teachings. Knowledge opens doors of opportunity you never thought possible. You are learning this, just in these last few weeks. I long to give you the riches of this world that will help to affect change for the good. You are nearer to spiritual things then you have ever been. Isn't it exciting? You are stopping the first vestiges of fear effectively. That is the biggest snare of the devil. Like a net, it catches up emotions and produces anxiety, unrest, and emotional upheaval. All of this delights the devil. Don't go there.

March 26

That Extra Effort When Weary

Because you are giving your best and putting out that extra effort, others are being touched. It is that sacrifice when you are least up to it in the flesh that shows Me you are sincere in pleasing Me. Remember what I told you that, as to an earthly father, you might say *look Dad what I have done.* You should view each task accomplished this way and, yes, I am smiling down on you with pleasure. I know you can feel that in your spirit. Rejoice in it as it is pleasing to both Me and to My Father.

March 27

Stand Firm

I desire that you should be aware that even your simplest prayers are being answered. I promised you that your burden would be light and your yoke easy. When you experience even the slightest frustration (worry) it shows a lack of faith and physically it is taxing to you. This is not necessary. My desire is to please My loved ones. I can easily do this. Stand firm on MY Word. It is living proof of My existence. It was given to build up the faith of My believers, give strength, spiritual knowledge, and comfort to the downhearted.

March 28

Live Life to the Fullest

See the wonders of My Father's hand. Find joy and awe in them. Each day is new, unlike any another, just as each personality or fingerprint is unique. Your life is changing from moment to moment, never static. Leap into life, don't choose to luxuriate in it too long.....Live it. Like a child, never loose that sense of wonderment. Enjoy each small moment. Savor its flavor. Find beauty in all you see and meet. Look for it if you must. It is there and will make you smile. Love all and it becomes easier. You know what I mean. You are seeing this and now laugh more easily and from the heart. I delight in your pleasure. Yes, I smile on you and yours, do not doubt it.

March 29

Avoid Vanity Seek Humility

Each breeze is My warm embrace. Treasure it as I treasure you. There is nothing I would not give you if it is for your good or betterment. It must be in keeping with what is right and pure. Vanity is to be avoided, humility sought after like precious gold. All are at various stages in their life's journey. Some are able to grow faster than others and reach new heights daily as you are doing now. It can be very exciting as you are finding out. I strive to keep your burden light and to renew your strength as it is needed. Your prayers are reaching Me and I answer them gladly. You are thankfully becoming aware of this. Your spiritual eyes are being opened. Your gratefulness for this is evident. You are hungrily seeking spiritual knowledge and that foundation, which you've formed over your life, is now being added to. Savor knowledge and truth for with it you can open doors for others to step into. In so doing you are widening their horizons, giving hope, and courage to help them move to new heights physically, emotionally, and spiritually. The latter being the most important of all.

March 30

No More Tears Cling to My Promises

You've just read that book that affirms you will see your loved ones in heaven, even animals, just as I've said and shown you in a vision. Even the sister you never met lost to your parents at birth will be there to greet you. Your parents are with her now and elated at the chance to be united. No more tears except of happiness, that is My promise. Cling to this and the hope of life everlasting. You will experience indescribable beauty with all of those you love including Me and My heavenly father. What more could you ask?

March 31

Spread My Joy

From glory to glory, I am taking you. Just as I promised, you are beginning to see the fruits of your labor. Listen, heed My voice, and follow My leading. You are planting many seeds. You will see them coming to harvest. Others not, but I see your efforts and smile upon you at your obedience. Their hearts are being softened by that initial contact. You are spreading the joy I have given you. Others can't help but pass it on. Giving in abundance causes others to desire to share the pleasure it brings. Give, give, give and it will be returned to you many times over.

April 1

A Joyful Reunion

Pain and sorrow are present here on earth and are a part of life. If you persevere, you will experience only joy and exuberance in the time called eternity. Patience and endurance are rewarded with pleasures too plentiful and grand for you to even imagine in heaven. Do not worry about your loved ones as I have kept My promises. They are and have been close to Me. They are here and waiting to greet you in the not too distant future. That is when you will experience the '*joy unspeakable*' I talk about in My word. They are all so eager to tell you how proud they are of you and show you their intense love. It will be a heartfelt reunion like none other ever on earth.

April 2

Rejoice in What is to Come

The pets that you choose to live with you are a way I show My love. You return it by caring for them with respect, kindness, and love. It is another way I help you to learn to give. Their antics, displayed in their individual personalities, bring pleasure, laughter, and delight which in turn brings Me happiness to see you are blessed by their presence. They, as well, await the ones they were so loyal to in life. Yes, another future joyful reunion awaits when your pets will recognize and greet you with the pleasure you and they have always felt toward one another. That is why I showed you the vision of a heaven with your loved ones caring for your beloved pets....Otherwise you would have continued to carry your depression. Yes, depression is like a heaviness. When it disappeared you felt as though the weight had been lifted. Pets are destined to live shorter lives so you will be exposed to the sadness of their loss many times if you choose to replace them when they die. Do not carry this sadness in your daily life as it does color all you do in darkness. Satan finds delight in your depression and sadness. Picture the glorious garden I have for them. Your loved ones are caring for these pets until you arrive. How then can you continue to be sad?

April 3

Your Need for One Another

Your fellowship with like minded Christians has strengthened your faith but also further linked you in the type of family atmosphere I encourage. Helping and uplifting one another in times of hardship as well as in those times of celebration is what I have always desired for you. Yes, there is strength in numbers, but more than that it is the encouragement you all need in this life which presents new challenges daily. Realization that the human condition requires trials for all and that many have already experienced them, helps those currently being put to the test to find the support needed through others. The joy is then multiplied when they have faced these trials and met with success. As you all rejoice together with the recipient you joyfully relive the experience again through them. This could be a wedding, birth of a child, a job promotion or any other life experience that you all have lived at one time or another. I am there rejoicing or comforting you as needed so that your spirits can soar to new heights.

April 4

Be an Encouragement to Others

Encouragement is what all of you need at one time or another. That you long to be that for others, and with such a loving heart, is what is at the core of being Christ like. Opportunities are being presented to you. You are facing the challenges with a renewed courage. I am with you and strengthen you when you feel weak or not up to the task. I am here to increase your strength daily in full measure when needed. To go the extra mile for Me is the ultimate sacrifice and, though the flesh is weak, you are not giving in to it when tempted. I honor that and your commitment to Me.

April 5

Speak Kind Words

Guard your tongue for with it you can offend so easily or cause hurt that can have detrimental consequences. Rumors, bullying, and hateful gossip have caused more sadness, heartache, and even death to those negatively affected by them. Seek to uplift others whenever given the chance and to find the good when it seems easier to find fault. The tongue, one small muscle, can wreak so much havoc. It can cause irreparable damage. Guard it with sacred care as the blessings it can bestow are a treasure more valuable then the most precious of jewels.

April 6

Hang on to Your Faith

Happiness is so within your grasp daily as you walk closer to Me. Your acknowledgement frees Me to bless you abundantly and, through you, bless others. You have been hot and cold for so long and now remain faithful. All must reach that point of surrender or be constantly plagued by the devil as he knows the flesh is weak. With such promptings as *you don't need to go to church*, or *sleep in you deserve it*, or *if you buy that it will fill that need.* So many search to fill a void that is a mystery to them. But when, at last, they reach for Me all becomes so evident. Then the reality of the ever present spiritual world becomes more valuable. The earthly things pass away without regret. It is such a struggle to get to this point. Some never do which is a pity. Such joy is available to everyone. It is My wish for all. You were made to fellowship with Me first. All else comes to you as a result of this. You are to be a blessing and comfort to others in this life. The challenges presented are to aide you in your spiritual growth. The ruler of this world seeks to distract you from your heavenly plan. He leads many to self destruction. Look at the damage alcohol and tobacco have done to this temple of the Holy Spirit, not to mention depression, fear, and addictions. Is it such a wonder so many go astray? It is the job of My people to shepherd them back to Me, the ones who cannot or will not heed My voice. Then I can say *well done My faithful servant* to those who encourage others to follow Me or plant the seeds of faith one at a time.

April 7

Invite Them to Come

We are coming upon the remembrance of My last days (Easter) and the celebration is world wide, yet the harvest is at hand and My laborers are few. The Holy Spirit can do mighty things when met with a ready heart. Do as you and your fellow Christians have been asked in obedience. I will reveal My wonders. I will bring the tired and weary to the holy tabernacle to drink of the water I offer freely to all who desire it.

April 8

Wait Expectantly

When you hear the first birds of the morning, think of them singing My love songs to you. It is the little things you pay the least attention to through which I try to gain your notice. It is when you are asleep, that you are closest to the spiritual world. Many profound thoughts, dreams, and visions come this way. Be open to this and have a pen ready to help you record these events. There are other ways that I am able to get your attention and lead you. The distractions of the world separate us making it more difficult for Me to reach you. Be attuned knowing I long to commune with you and wait expectantly. Make time to spend quietly with Me away from the world's demands. You will never regret it.

April 9

Heavenly Conversation

I've spoken about the value of prayer but more than that the simple act of listening for My voice. I esteem this above all. For what good is a one-way conversation? So many come to Me in supplication and, as a loving father, I strive to fill the needs. But, I desire the satisfaction of meeting with you in your quiet time to share precious moments during your otherwise busy day. You have discovered some of your best ideas during those times. Did you not know it was I whispering to you sharing My plans for you? Listen and converse with Me, I await.

April 10

My Presence Brings Joy

So many view a relationship with Me as tedious, rule bound, and lacking in pleasure. They look at earthly pleasures as of paramount importance. This is where I say *the flesh is weak.* Our earthly bodies crave satisfaction not knowing the ultimate joy of a spirit filled life. These earthly pleasures take on an even deeper enjoyable meaning when shared with Me. Those not Godly fall away easily. As with an earthly father who would delight in spending a day with his son or daughter, would he heap undesirable tasks upon his children or shower them with blessings?

April 11

Reach Out to Others

Help care for those who cannot fend for themselves. They are out there and need encouragement and love. Rather than become dependent on you, they become more self sufficient. Sometimes a simple kindly gesture is enough to renew their strength. Loving words give hope. They are like verbal rays of sunshine. Spread joy. Refrain from complaining. Others will desire to be in your presence.

April 12

Be Content in all Circumstances

Even in hardships, I am with you and will hold you up. Do not give in to negative emotions. Be content in whatever circumstance you encounter as these moments will pass quickly enough. Be calm in Me. Seek My council. The wisdom to proceed in the right direction or with choice words will be within your command. Just lean on Me. I will give the needed strength and knowledge to guide you.

April 13

Abolish Guilt

There is therefore now no condemnation to those who are in Christ Jesus, who do not walk according to the flesh, but according to the spirit. Romans 8:1

It is easy to feel guilt about the past and carry this as chains, forever tormenting you. I, in My sacrifice, freed you of this. I was made sin so your sin could be forgiven. Now cast it away from your thoughts into the deepest sea as I have. It is your choice whether to dredge it up over and over again. If I have forgotten it, shouldn't you? Claim the joy I have promised you if you have Me in your heart. This should be enough. I've given you the strength to carry today's burdens. I do not expect you to carry yesterday's or tomorrow's as well. Go in My peace with the assurance of My love. I give My total forgiveness if you have, indeed, repented with a humble and contrite heart.

April 14

Worship Me with Joy

I spoke against legalism in the Bible. So many religions today set such strict standards that it is not a pleasure to worship Me but a chore. Man often turns My simplicity into complex laws and rules or mindless ritual causing fear, anxiety, and confusion. The Bible is for all to read, to understand prior happenings and how to live a Godly life. It has been kept from many for too long and now is the most widely read book. All should seek to study and learn more of Me and My father's kingdom as it was, is now, and will be. This study is best done with others in an environment that fosters learning. Most churches offer Bible studies. Just relating to one another with a prayerful heart can open the Holy Spirit to reveal My truths. You have found where you belong. Others must seek to find a church that suits them. I will lead them to it through prayer if it is the honest desire of their hearts. They should seek to find a place where they feel welcome, ministered to, and can grow spiritually. It is this heart knowledge that I will give them to affirm this.

April 15

Indescribable Joy and Beauty Await You

As you are reminded of My sufferings, be aware of the heavenly rewards that were awaiting Me. It is so with you. Bare well your earthly burdens. In your efforts to keep My commandments, while drawing others to Me through your life and testimony, be constantly in prayer. It is a covering of protection over you preventing the penetration of evil to your fleshly body. Your spirit is then protected. Know that indescribable beauty awaits you. You will be rewarded immeasurably. Rejoice and draw strength from this knowledge.

April 16

Reveal a Heart For God

Have a heart for others. They cannot help but see, acting honorably when they might have done otherwise. Show your love. They cannot resist being drawn to you. If not, *"shake the dust from your feet"* as I advised My apostles. Go forth with renewed strength for there are so many others that are receptive. They are in need of a touch from Me.

April 17

Do this in Remembrance of Me

And he took bread, gave thanks and broke it, and gave it to them, saying, "This is My body which is given for you; do this in remembrance of Me." Luke: 22: 19

Holy communion is a sacred tradition I asked to have reenacted to remind you of My love for each of you and the sacrifice I made to assure you of My ultimate forgiveness of your past sins. Strive to sin not. Your very life is a sacrifice if lived with kindness, compassion, forgiveness, and love. I will draw ever closer to you daily as you strive to learn more of Me and follow My ways. Those who see Me in you are indeed blessed.

April 18

Guard the Treasures of Heart and Soul

Honor My words. They are as gold to an impoverished heart. What need have you of earthly things? You are of the spiritual world. Desire only those things that you must have to exist. Anything else is a blessing but can be in excess. Beware of becoming attached to material goods that wear out and become useless. Treasures of the heart and soul never tarnish and become more glowing with maturity. Cherish these as you do your loved ones.

April 19

That First Step

As your soul thirsts for Me, others seek but cannot find Me. Be a beacon to them gently leading them to My living water. The first step is often one in many. To place their feet firmly on that first step can be your goal. When I bring a person to your remembrance, it is to serve a need in them. I will guide you in prayer in what you are to do or say. Be not weary, I will direct you in every instance if only you will heed My still small voice or that of the Holy Spirit. It is like a gentle nudging. You have felt it but not realized it as that. Then you have followed through and been doubly blessed. You are recognizing the truth in what I say as you have experienced it often.

IN PRAISE OF HIM

April 20

What You Mean to Me

Your mercies are many, your grace undeniable, your love unfathomable. I adore you from the depths of my soul. My songs and praises cannot do justice for all You have been to me. My greatest desire is that Your face smiles upon me as I try to follow Your ways, my precious Father, heavenly savior. I savor Your presence and glorify Your name for all to see the wonders of Your marvelous works.

April 21

In Awe of You

How mysterious are Your ways. In all that I know, I am constantly amazed at the wondrous things You do. There is none like You who touches the very heart of my being. You cause me joy indescribable. To repay all of Your kindnesses could occupy me forever. Yet I would do it gladly. I am in awe of You and Your divine works. All I ask is that you guide me, all the days of my life, until I have the ultimate pleasure of being in your presence. I await this glorious day and fear not for I know You are with me today and always to eternity.

April 22

Your Sacred Protection

You protect me from my enemies when they are all around me and I am unaware. For this I am forever grateful. As the poison darts of the enemy fly, you catch them in your nail scarred hands. For this I give you praise. You do the same for my loved ones. Your mercies are abundant. I will praise you to the end of my days with words of adoration on my dying lips, dear Lord.

April 23

You are Ever Faithful

You have healed my body and my love starved soul. Your mighty hand has kept my path straight when I have gone astray so many times. Your faithfulness is my anchor when I have been so far from You. You are forever loyal keeping each promise with truth and integrity. I strive to share a portion of your goodness as I go about my daily tasks. Continue to show Me, your humble servant, your heavenly ways so that I may reflect the beauty of your countenance.

April 24

We are Adored and Cherished

What would you have me do to show my love for You? Nothing compares to the sacrifice You endured to secure for us a place with your heavenly Father. No matter that so many have turned from You, You remain faithfully awaiting their humble acknowledgement. Forgetting past sins, You accept us as we are, undeserving of Your mercy, grace, and kindnesses. What more could anyone ask then to be adored and cherished as You do us? You are always ready to take us back when we have strayed, receiving us as the father did his prodigal son in the well known Bible story, with a joyous and forgiving heart. You are ever ready to lavish blessings upon us despite our shortcomings. Your loving kindness is beyond measure.

April 25

I Stand in Awe of You

The genius and mystery of all Your creation is beyond comprehension. Each equipped to survive in its own unique way. From the simplest of plants to all the species of insects, animals, sea creatures and more, we can see the marvels of our universe. Your wisdom is such that all are able to survive in environments suited to them blending in, where needed, for protection. Man got to name them but You, in Your infinite wisdom, created them once more demonstrating Your power and genius. I will ever stand in awe of You.

April 26

Hope for Eternity

View the warm sun as an embrace. The gentle wind a hug. Its sound and those of the birds My love songs to You. Commune with Me. You will partake of these and so much more. Seek the quiet times in your busy world. In those I can more easily communicate, through My Word, but also in the beauty that surrounds you. Take the time to enjoy what I have prepared for you here on earth knowing that what awaits you is incomparable. With the promise of so much more, even the heaviest of burdens of this life can be born with this hope I've instilled in your heart and soul.

April 27

Holy Spirit

My words are a balm for the weary soul. It is My hope you find solace in these and in the Bible, a legacy for all. It is intended to teach, reveal, bring healing, and draw you even closer to My father and Me. The Holy Spirit is your guide. Seek Him to lead you in all you do and He will bring you into a deeper relationship. It is that easy for, as I promised, the living water revives, energizes, and gives renewed hope and healing.

April 28

Love One Another

I am the alpha and omega, the beginning and the end. Sitting at the right hand of My father, I rule and reign with Him. Nothing supersedes our power and majesty. The ruler of this earth shudders at the mention of My name. The fact that evil coexists with good here is contrary to the plan of God, bringing death and destruction where beauty and goodness should be paramount. Darkness lurks where only light should permeate the atmosphere here. In its shadows exists fear, anxiety, sadness, depression, sickness, regret, guilt, remorse, discrimination, and hatred. If I had My way, I would wave My mighty hand over the land to bring it all back to what was intended in the beginning. But free will was always the plan of My father and with it comes greed, envy, lust for power, pride, and selfishness. The all encompassing love once permeating this earth has slowly eroded but still exists in a select few. Its radiance can once again conquer the evil prevailing here. Bear one another up in hardship, stay the course, pass on kindnesses bestowed upon you, and cling to the hope eternal of a better world to come. Love one another as I have loved you knowing good overcomes evil.

April 29

Desire to Dine at My Table

You have just dipped your foot into the ocean of My love. I long to cover you if you were but to ask. So few know the extent of My deep longing to be a part of their lives and to be acknowledged. That is why it has always been a choice, free will, available to all. The open invitation to dine at My table is forever offered.

Heavenly food is so much more satisfying then the earthly. My living water never leaves a soul thirsty once tasted. Desire more and it will be granted.

April 30

I Will Lead You

If only you knew how I have guided you when you knew not where to turn, what to say, or how to act. My protection over you has kept you safe and under My wing when the enemy sought to take you out. The prayers of others for you and your desire to learn more of Me have drawn you closer to Me. Continue in the direction you have chosen. I will clasp your hand in Mine to lead you into a deeper relationship. Dispelling fear has opened so many more doors than you can imagine and slammed shut an opening for the devil to gain access to your soul. So much hardship could have been avoided if you had grasped some of My simple precepts earlier in life. Cling to My truths, many Biblical, others I've spoken to you in your quiet times. You will flourish like a well tended tree, its branches stretching upward and outward bearing the best of fruit for all to see and taste.

May 1

Embrace all Circumstances

Pain and sorrow will always be a part of life if you allow yourselves to love. With it comes refining. What would you know of joy in contrast if you were not tried? What if you had not passed through life's flames? Embrace all circumstances realizing that through these trials you are growing, maturing, and becoming stronger as the trunk of a mighty tree must support its branches and fruit. I give you all you need to endure. My grace is sufficient for all your needs. Go forward with strength, confidence and hope in Me. It is My pleasure to carry you when needed. Go, My Beloved, and prove yourself.

May 2

The Highest Calling

Rejoice in each new day, a new beginning, an adventure. Go forth with renewed energy, courage, love, and a sense of awe at the challenges before you. To reach others for Me is the highest calling. I have prepared you more fully each day. Cover yourself with the full armor of God, the helmet of salvation, the breastplate of righteousness, the belt of truth, the sandals of peace, the shield of faith and the sword of My word. Fully prepared for battle, the enemy stands no chance before you. Go forth in boldness, My chosen one, and fear not for I stand beside you to uphold and protect you.

May 3

Rejoice in Daily Gifts

Just as the new buds of spring show themselves, life is renewed daily through sleep. A small miracle each day but unnoticed. So many require a sign. How many more of My daily blessings need be unveiled that you take heed that I am forever with you? The signs are everywhere from the star filled skies, to the never still ocean. Embrace My presence by inhaling the fresh smells of the forest or a newly opened flower. Signs of Me and My Father's love are all about you. Rejoice in these daily gifts given gladly to all of creation but seldom acknowledged by a mere "thank you Lord." We have all seen an ungrateful child whose desires can never be satisfied. Haven't you been like that at one time or another? Be mindful of what you have. Give thanks daily. It is a mere pittance in comparison to what is in store for you if you but follow My ways and have a heart for Me.

May 4

A Prayerful Heart

Face all with a prayerful heart filled with songs of praise. I sing to you, as well, if you listen. I wish only gladness and cheer in a world often beset with sadness and regret. How I long to heal the hurts of My people. It must often be done though others appointed by Me for the task. Be open and aware of those about you. I've given you a sensitive heart to know their needs. I long to draw them near to Me. Kind words are a healing balm. You can be a part of that. The satisfaction you will get is My blessing to you. Cherish it as it means more to Me than the highest praise. You are anointed to be used of Me. Tarry not for the workers are few. The needs are so many.

May 5

I Hear Your Sighs

How I long to take you in My arms and comfort you through the hard times of life. The Holy Spirit can intercede for Me and quench the spirit of sadness. As I promised He is with you to lead, comfort, and convey My power in times of need. Harness this as you would any form of energy needed to proceed through your day. Believe as you conceive of the tasks you need to perform. Each step will be ordered and sure. No need to worry or give place for fear. That is just what the enemy desires. It is a sure stumbling block to your success. With a prayerful heart and spirit seek council. Your prayers will be heard and answered. My promises to you, found in the Bible, are your guarantee of My faithfulness.

May 6

Seek My Face

My ever faithful one, if ever you truly knew the depths of My love. I have sought you when you were seeking Me and did not know it. Those lonely times of despair were not lost to Me. I have been loyal, it is you who needed to find the way to Me. I sent others to guide you when you most needed them. In your darkest moments I was there. You felt My presence. Your hope was renewed. I allowed you to lean on Me for strength. My promise to never leave or forsake you is real. I never said you would not leave Me as you have done in the past. Our relationship is more stable now. It can only deepen if you continue to seek My face.

May 7

My Peace is Your Covering

Continue to seek Me. What you desire will come to pass. I know your wants and needs even better than you do. You are developing more patience to wait on Me. It is an instant world with often unrealistic expectations. So many know not what they want, never satisfied with their lot. You, My dear one, are getting closer. That is why the way seems more difficult, the challenges like ocean waves coming one after another. It does get easier. Hold fast to My promise of the peace that passes all understanding. It is there in abundance. Just ask when your burdens seem more than you can bear. I long to satisfy your every need without you having to ask. I often do. If only you could understand this, you would be so encouraged. I would have you to know this. I go before you and yours guarding and protecting as you have wished. Have no fear. The outcome is what you would desire for your loved ones.

May 8

Speak the Wisdom I Impart

You are such an encouragement to others and are heeding My voice at the right moment. How does it make you feel? Now you know how proud I am of you. I have placed a new wisdom and boldness within you. Use it wisely for, as I've said, your words can brighten the darkened world, your encouragement bolster a burdened heart. I would that you go forth as you have already done with more boldness and with a sincere heart. Yes, they are seeing Me in you. You are being blessed with a lightened heart and lifted spirit. They are as well. Thank you for being obedient. It is My pleasure to call you Mine.

May 9

Cover them with Prayer

Continue to cover your loved ones, and those others you care so deeply for in prayer. Your prayers beam up to waiting emissaries, angels with a mission to conquer enemy forces. They are ever ready to act on your requests and hasten to do My will. Be heartened that they go forth with My power and My Father's blessings to accomplish all that is needed. Rest in that peace. Assure those who need it that this is so. A willing vessel can bring forth victory by being obedient and patient. You have prepared yourself well over these many years. Doubt not that I have been watching. I am well pleased. You have shown yourself approved. Your crown is waiting.

May 10

I Reward My Faithful Ones

I have a name for you in heaven and shall reveal it to you soon. You will not have to wait. I long to reward you with it early. Shall I not be an encouragement to you as you have been to others? You have felt much earthly pain and endured. Your being has been strengthened by it. I have molded you in an image closer to My own. I am not done with you. As you seek intimacy with Me, I am drawing even closer. Yes, the pattern of your life is unfolding a step at a time, but all the steps have been ordered by Me through your obedience. I reward My faithful ones.

May 11

Desire More and it Will be Granted

In the darkest of days strive to find the light of My glory within yourself. Look from whence you have come to the mystery of it all. It will be gradually unfolded. Nothing happens by chance but is instead a testing, as a fine metal is brought through the forge. Without the hottest of temperatures the true beauty cannot shine forth. Magnify the greatest pain and suffering in your life and you will hardly come close to what I had to endure at Calvary. My arms outstretched were to attest to My sacrifice in love for all mankind. It exists today and extends to all of creation, radiating out upon the earth. If only those so close to it would seek to know Me. Many search in all the wrong places experiencing frustration and despair. If only they would seek Me in quiet prayer and meditation, they would experience the full measure of what I have to give.

May 12

Heaven on Earth

I long to provide a heaven here on earth, just a taste of what is to come. Look about you for all I have provided. Think not of lack but rather the multitude of blessings already provided. Speak out words of beauty. These go forth as beams of light, spreading love and hope further than you know. You will not want for anything if I am to have My way. As a loving father, I will meet your needs even before you are aware of them. I've kept the enemy away without your knowledge and stand ready to defend your boundaries. My power and your obedience can go far in expanding My kingdom. Seek Godly wisdom, the knowledge to do right in all situations. I provide answers through the prayer of a diligent heart.

May 13

A Joyful Heart

Draw others unto you through kind words, deeds, and a Godly manner. These are irresistible to those who are lost. Like a healing balm applied to the body, they nurture a spirit who is seeking. Refreshed as from a deep slumber, those you minister to rise up with renewed hope. Caring one for another deeply from a heart of love blesses abundantly both the one who gives and the receiver. I am the model of this kind of giving which leaves a joyful heart as the result.

May 14

Seek My Presence

I am always here for you with the wisdom you seek. Ask as you would an earthly father. Dispel the negative thoughts of the enemy. As you know once they have a foothold it is difficult to be rid of them. My blessings are freely given daily. Be aware of this and seek them. Choose to be happy. Your joy is My aim but it is your free will to choose it. So many go astray down negative paths of destruction of their own making. With My help you can create a heaven on earth until that time when you experience it in actuality. Hold fast to your hopes and dreams. I am always here to help you attain them.

May 15

I Treasure All

Each dear heart, all of creation, is treasured by Me. All are equal in My eyes. Strive not to judge others in light of this. All are given opportunities to live to their fullest abilities. Their possibilities are endless to the farthest reaching depths of their imaginations. As you are discovering, there are no limits. Strive, reach, desire, go forward but never back. All is yours and within your grasp. I have been preparing you these many years. All of your steps have been ordered but, you laid the foundation by being obedient.

May 16

Pray Daily

Guard all I have given you in prayer daily. I send My ministering angels, although you have not been aware of this. Those dear to Me, obedient and true, reap both earthly and heavenly rewards. Accept them with a grateful heart. Let praise be on your lips for I have truly blessed you and yours abundantly more than you know.

May 17

Leave a Negative Atmosphere

Rejoice, be outwardly joyful with a countenance that exudes the pleasure you are experiencing. Do not let others mar this joy. Leave if the atmosphere becomes negative. Yes, you will be affected and need not be. Hold fast to the blessings I bestow. Forbid others to steal your joy, no matter what. Your happiness is a healing balm for body, soul, and mind. It is My fondest wish for you. Your laughter brings Me great pleasure.

IN PRAISE OF HIM

May 18

Your Ambassador

Let my wisdom come forth as a blessing to others through Your leading, My Lord. I desire to bridle my sometimes careless tongue, being slow to speak and quick to pick up on Godly wisdom. Let me not hurt others through my words or actions. As a bright shining light or a warm embracing breeze let my countenance leave others refreshed and energized. I look to Your strength, Lord, to shore me up on wings of eagles when, otherwise, my spirit becomes weary with the weight of worldly cares. Let me become more attuned to Your holy spirit and to His leading knowing when to speak and when to remain silent. I seek, beyond all, to bring hope, encouragement, joy, and fresh knowledge to those who seek it, being a blessing as Your ambassador.

May 19

Ministering Angels

I am here to carry you when you cannot bear life's burdens. I will lift you up to greater heights when you cling to My everlasting promises. I have placed My ministering angels around you to comfort, strengthen, encourage, and protect you. They are a buffer against the evil intended by the enemy. Trust that they have been sent by Me and form a hedge around you and those you care for.

May 20

I Am Ever With You

My Word brings solace to the troubled, hope to the down hearted, and faith to the faithless. Far more valuable then food, the Bible satisfies spiritual hunger for those who seek Me there. Yet I am closer to you then this for I dwell in the hearts of those who love Me. I am easily summoned as needed. 'Emmanuel', the God who is with you, should be your solace and encouragement.

May 21

His Song for me

(To the tune of 'You Raise Me up')

When you are sad and troubles seem so many
Know that I'm here and share in all your pain
So just cry out to Me and in an instant
I'll comfort you and hold you once again

Chorus

I'm your strong shield and ever your protector
The one who helps you weather every storm
I give My strength to overcome your weakness
Beside you always to carry you along.

So wipe those tears go forth with renewed courage
You have the wisdom fortitude and might
to conquer all the enemy's slings and arrows
for you are covered by Me both day and night

Chorus (see above)

Life brings so many trials and tribulations
To test and strengthen and bring you close to Me
Praise Me in all, even the deepest heartaches
To know someday you'll ever dwell with Me.

Chorus

May 22

No More Tears

Yes, hurt and heart are just two letters different yet we experience our deepest hurts within our hearts, hence the words heartache and heartsick. Our hearts and minds are connected through our emotions which are linked to our memories. Tears are the means by which you can rid yourself of inward pain. They are the release I have given you to vent those unavoidable emotions. Although tears are a healthy outlet in moderation, when not put in check they can trap you in a cycle of self pity that is harmful. Tears are a helpful emotional outlet but, as with anything else in excess be it gluttony, foul language, drinking, and drugs to name a few, can be damaging if not kept in moderation, Yes, in the Bible it says '*Jesus wept*, and I did for My dear friend Lazarus. But for many, later, those tears shed became happy tears. Sadness was turned to joy. My wish is to do this for you whenever possible. I long to bring joy in place of tears, laughter in place of sighs and weeping. I prepare a place for you where there are no more tears, but rest, rejoicing, and beauty beyond measure. Words become insufficient to describe the glory I have planned for you. Keep your eyes heavenward for from there comes your reward.

May 23

I'll Sing to You

Just as you could write a song for Me, I have written a song for you. (See May 21) And someday I will sing to you as you have sung to Me on earth. Look forward to that day when I can let you know your worth to Me. You will be amazed at the wonder of it.

May 24

Care for the Neediest of Them

Think of the times when you are most content with no thought of any needs or chores to be done. I give you those times to recharge and rest your body. An amazing instrument, the human body, giving beyond measure and, for the most part, able to perform for many years that required of it. The plan of the Master is a work of perfection, but not always. In those times it is for others to help care for the needy. In so doing you are serving Me. This does not go unnoticed or unrewarded. That you would do for another to feed, cloth, shelter, and teach is as if you do it unto Me. Treat these, My special ones, with respect, love, and patience. In so doing you perfect your character. As I have said, all are equal in My sight no matter the physical or mental challenges. Love and acceptance crosses all boundaries to create a full life for the recipient. I increase the blessings of those who minister to them.

May 25

Dispel Fear with Love

Your fears are so often unfounded. You let them overtake you and bring you down. I have emphasized that fear is of the enemy. It is used relentlessly to hurt My loved ones and steal from them the richness of life. Do not fall for the wiles of the devil. Picture the smiling face of evil each time fear appears. It hurts you in all areas physically, mentally, and spiritually. For, in giving in to fear, you put that smile on his face and are pulled away from Me. Remember My promises concerning fear: *You, dear children, are from God and have overcome them, because the one who is in you is greater than the one who is in the world.* (John 4:4) *The Lord is my light and my salvation; Whom shall I fear? The Lord is the strength of my life; Of whom shall I be afraid?* (Psalm 27:1), *The fear of man brings a snare, But whoever trusts in the Lord shall be safe.* (Proverbs 29:25), *For God has not given us a spirit of fear, but of power and of love and of a sound mind.* (2nd Timothy 1:7), *There is no fear in love, but perfect love casts out fear, because fear involves torment. But he who fears has not been made perfect in love.* (1st John 4:18)

May 26

The Word is Your Sword

There is power in scripture. Use it as a vital tool, a weapon for battle. It is the sword I have provided to protect and instruct you. Commit as many verses as you can to memory. Store them in your heart for there will come a time when you will need them. The Holy Spirit will bring them to your remembrance when the time arrives. Bathe your spirit in the living Word. You will never thirst or hunger for anything in this world. My promises will not be found null or void.

May 27

Love the Greatest Gift

I give you love to share with others and for them to share with you. It is the glue that binds, the joy of life. It yields the best of what life has to offer. In your creation plan it was My father's purpose to shower you with love from every corner of your life to bring security, comfort, and just a small portion of what is in store for you in eternity. Imagine a thousand fold the greatest love of your life. You will not come close to what My father offers you in heaven. Be obedient, loving, kind, do good works, and hold the course no matter how rocky. You will receive your heart's desires even though you may not know what they are right now, I do.

May 28

I Will Not Fail You

Have I not shown you My loving care, fulfilled some of your greatest desires, and answered many of your fervent prayers? I'll not fail you if you put your trust in Me. I will give you a peace to handle daily hurdles which you never thought possible. Look with renewed hope and faith as you face each new day that I will provide for all your needs and guide you in all you do. Look to Me when you are in doubt or need to make a decision before you blindly rely on man. I am here for you and desire to give you a rich life of abundant blessings. As it is written *My yoke is easy and My burden light.* (Matthew 11:30).

May 29

Holy Reunion

How can anyone doubt the love I have for them? It is as deep as a mother's or father's love for their child or a child's love for a parent. It is deeper than you know or have ever experienced for you see, you are My father's creation, a part of Me. As one of Mine draws closer to Me, I in turn become more intimate with them. I will not force you although sometimes I give a nudge. For when you make that choice I and My angels rejoice as it is a holy reunion, one that touches the heart, spirit, and soul of us and you. Nothing comes closer to this then when you return home to your heavenly Father to be reunited with Him and your loved ones.

May 30

Never Give Up

Never give up in trying to reach others for Me. Besides acknowledging Me each day in thought, prayer, and communication, your ultimate goal should be to reach others for Me. So many need Me or a renewed hope in Me that every waking hour would not reach all who are in need. My angels, the Holy Spirit, and others are reaching many as well so it is not an impossible task. To be given the choice and reject it is a heartbreak for Me, but a reality. When our loved ones are cruel or reject us it is the deepest of hurts to experience, as you well know. When I have given the ultimate sacrifice for mankind out of love for all no matter the sin, to be ignored or rejected is devastating. I am not a stranger to pain, hatred, and rejection. I faced it before My crucifixion, even by My beloved apostle Judas and Peter who denied knowing Me three times as I suffered going to and on the cross. You, as well, will face rejection in My name. When you do remember that this is a cross you will have to bear to follow Me, but it is worth it. You will be rewarded in the end, My ever faithful one.

May 31

Your Steps are Ordered

The steps of a righteous man are ordered. Do not worry how the plan for your life will unfold. Your obedience and quiet times with Me in prayer, Bible reading, and fellowship with others of like mind will bring you further on your journey. I will bring it all to light. All will be evident at the right time. For now, trust in Me to lead the way, bring those to you who I have chosen, and develop the God-given talent that you have been given. I am well pleased in you. You are listening, acting, and speaking as an ambassador to Me.

June 1

Godly Fear, a Blessing Not a Curse

So many do not understand the phrase *fear of God.* My Father does not wish for His creation to fear Him. Rather the fear spoken of in the Bible is that of reverence and obedience. How can Christians claim to desire a Godly relationship if they pay lip service at church and, for example, lead a promiscuous life? Or take in many of the other worldly offerings that offend God. Even watching a movie or television show that portrays an immoral life style or uses profanity implies that the viewer agrees with or at least is able to condone what is being said or done. When My Father gave the Israelites the choice to come closer to Him in a more intimate relationship such as He shared with Moses, they refused. They were not willing to be obedient in all things in order to receive what would have been a blessing beyond all measure for them. If only they had known what might have been. When in doubt of whether you are in the right always ask *Father would you approve of this?* He will answer or place in your spirit the answer you require.

June 2

Give in Secret for True Fulfillment

Put Me first in your life. All else will fall into place. Not such an easy task for some. The flesh begs to be satisfied in so many ways. It is easy to become distracted by the world. As you have put Me first, you have been more easily led by the Holy Spirit when beckoned. You are reaching out in love and caring to others more than ever before and reaping the dividends. It is much more blessed to give than to receive. It is really you that benefits the most. When we turn from ourselves to others we become Godlier especially if we are humble and do not brag of our sacrifices just as in fasting. You are learning My dear one.

June 3

Make Time for Your Talents

I often just ask that those who love Me do what they love best. In doing this you can not only serve Me but reach others for Me. You see, if you are using your God-given talents you are fulfilled but also your temperament is such that your joy flows over to others. I have given unique gifts to all but many struggle in other endeavors and fail to use them. That is why they are frustrated. Often this keeps them from finding Me for I am drawing them closer through their talents. My workers long to please Me and can by recognizing My plan for their lives. Some find it easily but others are rebellious letting their fleshly needs exceed their true desires. I wish that, until that day when we meet in heaven, your earthly life is an adventure filled with love, joy, excitement, service to others, fellowship, and the awe of knowing you are truly loved by a heavenly Father who wants the best for you. Bask in this love and care for you as it is always within your grasp.

Available to All

June 4

<table>
<tr><td></td><td>L</td><td></td></tr>
<tr><td></td><td>I</td><td></td></tr>
<tr><td></td><td>F</td><td></td></tr>
<tr><td></td><td>E</td><td></td></tr>
<tr><td>JOY</td><td>SON</td><td>PEACE</td></tr>
<tr><td></td><td>F</td><td></td></tr>
<tr><td></td><td>O</td><td></td></tr>
<tr><td></td><td>R</td><td></td></tr>
<tr><td></td><td>G</td><td></td></tr>
<tr><td></td><td>I</td><td></td></tr>
<tr><td></td><td>V</td><td></td></tr>
<tr><td></td><td>E</td><td></td></tr>
<tr><td></td><td>N</td><td></td></tr>
<tr><td></td><td>E</td><td></td></tr>
<tr><td></td><td>S</td><td></td></tr>
<tr><td></td><td>S</td><td></td></tr>
</table>

June 5

Look for Opportunities

Opportunities abound in which to show My love daily. Be open to them as was the small boy with the fish and loaves who gave them to Jesus to feed the multitude. Imagine the joy he felt to report to his mother what he had seen that day. Look to each day expectantly that it will offer you a chance to be a blessing. You, My dear one, will be doubly blessed.

June 6

Open Your Spiritual Eyes

The richness of this world is nothing in comparison to what I offer. When those here take their eyes off what they think they need and open their eyes to the needs of others, a great step is taken in the right direction. I say feed My hungry for they are many and often suffer in silence. Cloth My weary and down trodden for a simple gesture blesses for many days to come. Shelter those who need protection for their needs can be the greatest when anxiety and fear enter in. Safety is of utmost importance before anything else. Keep your eyes open. I will show you those who need your touch. They surround you yet you are blind to them when you always think of your needs first. Ask for your spiritual eyes to be opened. I will do the rest if you will be My instrument. I thank you ahead of time for being obedient for, when you help care for My sheep, you are in essence caring for Me. All of My children are beloved by Me. My greatest desire is to save My lost. Some need but a gentle nudge in the right direction. It often takes few words and a right attitude to bring this to pass. Rely on the Holy Spirit for within you is the power to bring about positive change.

June 7

Choose Your Words Carefully

Your words, wisely chosen, can bring life and hope as you have seen more than once. You also have felt the sting of rejection and hurt through other's words. Remember this, be slow to react, and you will be more careful in what you say. The negative and positive can affect you either raising or depressing your spirit. Guard your hearts, minds, and spirits in what you allow yourselves to see and hear. As with your bodies, you would not knowingly imbibe harmful substances. Be slow to criticize or find fault. All are at various stages in their growth process as well as the circumstances of their lives, therefore always keep this in mind when you are trying to help. If unsure pray to Me to give them what they need as I am mindful of this. We are all connected to one another, so our joys and sufferings often overlap even those of strangers. Your body is a temple. Treat it well as it is not replaceable.

June 8

Pray for Others

It is hard to know the mind of others. Outside smiles can cover the deepest of hurts. Be aware of this and be sensitive to the feelings of those around you. Pray for them if you cannot find the words to comfort. I know their needs and will intercede for you. Prayer is one of My most powerful tools. Use it wisely. Much can be accomplished through it.

June 9

Your Struggles will Not Go Unrewarded

All of you are unique creations unto God. Each with equal value of supreme worth and divine potential. Do not question this for I will someday reveal these mysteries to you. Live life as fully as you can. Allow those in your care to do the same. Your struggles will not go unrewarded.

June 10

Be Obedient

The greatest gift you can give to your heavenly Father is to be obedient. Through this you gain intimacy with your creator. Be still, listen, worship, pray, and read My Word. I will fellowship with you. You will know if you are following My ways for I've given you a heart and spirit to discern this.

For God hath not given us a spirit of fear; but of power, and of love and of a sound mind. (2nd Timothy 1:7) Believe this and hold fast to your faith.

June 11

Be Aware of Opportunities

I've given you another day. Make it special. Put all of yourself into it to give in any way possible. As beautiful as it is, it is a hurting world out there. Be open to talk to those who come across your path. You might hold the key to giving them the hope that is offered to all. Don't miss your chance. I give you the words through the Holy Spirit. Just be patient. Let Me do the rest. I am pleased to bless you and those who need blessings through you.

June 12

Reach Out

Small acts of kindness send ripples through the universe. Like the person who saves one starfish at a time, tiny sacrifices reap many benefits in the end. Be ever mindful of what is happening about you. Opportunities abound to bring joy, smiles, and encouragement around every corner. You are already beginning to accomplish this with ease. Carry on. You will never regret reaching out. I am smiling upon you, My beloved.

June 13

I Give You Eternity

My time is not your time. Be not mindful of what you must accomplish for I give you eternity. In My universe fear, guilt, worry, sadness, sickness, and despair have no place. Only love, kindness, grace, patience, forgiveness, joy, thankfulness, and gladness should dwell here. Sometimes only prayer, fasting, and supplication, can bring about the changes needed to cause miracles to happen. Remember this, that when things seem at their worst, I am still in charge. I and My angels are ministering to bring about the necessary changes in heart, spirit, and occurrences to reflect My love. The stubborn wills of others can only be softened through patience, prayer, and the gentle prodding of the Holy Spirit. Free will is an entitlement. Through it others can be led to make the right choices. Be mindful that, in the end, they must make the ultimate choice. You may have made the slightest comment to plant that seed of faith for the next step to be taken. I am mindful of your efforts even when you do not see the fruit.

June 14

Choose Wisely

Let not dreary days dishearten you. They come as do unhappy thoughts or sad remembrances. Choose to entertain pleasant musings. You can create your own cheerful setting no matter what the circumstances. Your mindset is a personal choice as is what you select to eat or the company you keep. Choose wisely for you are what you allow into your life. Some choices can bring their own undesirable consequences. In all decisions seek Me in prayer and I will guide you if you take the time and effort to listen to My voice. I always desire the best for you.

June 15

Be a Light Unto Others

I have given you those to love and those who love you to make your journey here a pleasant one. Guard your words that they will never hurt others. Life here is hard in different ways for all of you and an unkind or a thoughtless word or gesture can bring with it the deepest of pain. Seek to uplift and edify all whom you meet. They will be drawn to you like a moth drawn to the light. The wisdom you have attained though your joys and hardships can be of benefit to others at the proper time. Be open to sharing as the need arises. Your trials and triumphs have prepared you in ways even you are not aware of. Your readiness to share at the right time can brighten lives and bring renewed hope. Be ever ready for those opportunities I bring to you.

June 16

Call Upon Me

Remain calm in all situations. A ruffled spirit leads to misspoken words, impaired judgement, and undue torment. Clarity of mind requires quiet composure. If you are not able to grasp this, pray to Me to give you the assurance you need. Remember I am never far from you. I desire to be used of you and called upon as you would an earthly father or mother.

June 17

Your Patience Will be Rewarded

As you and yours draw nearer to Me, you will undoubtedly come under attack from the enemy. If you remain faithful, obedient, and trust in Me through all, you will be amazed what blessings come though weathering these trials. It is during such times when your patience will be tested. Often it is better not to act but allow Me to go before you or your loved ones. Ask and I will guide you or tell you to be still. Let Me take control. Your discernment in these difficult times will be sharpened if you seek My wisdom. Count it all as spiritual growth, the pain of it well worth the sacrifice, to allow heaven's blessings to be poured out upon you and those you care for.

June 18

I Go Before You

I have no regard for time as you sense it. My timing is perfect, although you may not find this so. Too many expect instant answers as they would with the touch of a button or a fast food order. I will often bring you through a trial by your patience thus refining you like forged metal or baked clay. You cannot see to the other side of a situation. I will order the steps to bring victory in My time. If only you were aware of how often your prayers are answered. How quickly you forget even what you pray. Be reassured that I am in control. Let go of the situation so I can do the work. Allow the peace of knowing I will make your paths smooth to keep you calm and encouraged in your many trials.

June 19

Draw Closer to Me

What greater gift in life is there then My love for you? When others fail you I continue to steadfastly remain by your side to encourage, protect, and answer if you but listen and obey. It could be so easy for many to reach Me, yet they insist on holding fast to pride and arrogance when all I seek is a humble and contrite heart. The keys to My heart are humility and obedience. The desire to serve then follows and with it comes an intimacy with Me. As they draw nearer the blessings flow so naturally, it often amazes the recipients. Then the joy is difficult to contain. Their countenance changes, others see it and are attracted to them as they reflect Me, the One they are truly seeking. Sometimes the answers are right before them yet the world has them in blinders much like those of a horse. So set in their ways that My hands are tied to help them. The irony is heartbreaking to Me as I see and feel their pain and frustration.

June 20

Let Go of Those Suitcases

Do not hold on to past hurts, regrets, or heartaches. Even recalling their memories is like carrying heavy suitcases, the weight of which can weigh you down. Let them go as soon as you notice you are holding them. I give you each new day for a fresh beginning. I never expected you to carry the load of past or future troubles as well as the trials of today. Do not look back or ahead but rest in today. I give you the strength to carry but one day at a time. Face it with joy and expectancy. You will be surprised and pleased in what I can show you.

June 21

I Am a Prayer Away

I never expected for the human body to work 24/7 each day without resting, yet some put it to the test. Even your heavenly Father rested when done with creation. Your body is a temple, treat it with respect. Only you know if you are not for, others are too busy to pay heed to you. All that you see, eat, and expose yourself to are forming who and what you are. These things can become like a god or gods to you leading in the wrong direction and causing pain. Some see this too late. They can only regret the waste of a life, given over to bad habits and unfortunate choices. Seek My council if you are in doubt for I am but a prayer away.

June 22

You are Dear to Me

You were created to fellowship with others of like mind. Guard your dealings with the wrong crowd as you can become less like the self you admire. If in doubt give yourself thinking time to rearrange your priorities. Do not be a disappointment to yourself or to Me, who created you for better things. Avoid hurtful gossip by asking yourself, if it were me being talked about would I be offended. Even in jest, words can injure the human heart so easily. Guard your body, mind, heart, and spirit as you are, My precious creation, so dear to Me.

June 23

Be Open to Blessing Others

Service to others can bring such joy. It is often the last thing on your mind. In the rush of daily life even one kind word or a smile can brighten someone's day. Be mindful that others have trials just as you do. Strive to make their load a little easier. If you but knew the struggles of others, you would be so much more compassionate. Approach life in such a way that all you meet will find joy in your presence. It is not so hard if you are open to others. Listen beyond their words and actions.

June 24

Make Time for Enjoyment

Don't miss the beauty of nature by getting caught up in the mundane tasks of life. Make time to sit in the sunshine, walk in the forest, play with your pets in the grass, or visit a new and exciting place. Your days are shorter then you think. Reward yourself often for your struggles are many. You will find rest and rejuvenate your spirit in these small enjoyments. Take a different path, a new route, or seek out someone who would benefit from a visit or dinner invitation. You can bless others by being yourself and in return will be doubly blessed by those you minister to.

June 25

Time is a Gift

Give the gift of time. Be it a phone call, email, prayer for others, a visit, or letter. When you do this, a chain reaction is set off as the recipient often will reach out and play it forward so to speak. Like a rippling pond reacting to a stone's throw, the world is made a better place. I did this in My brief visit to earth, while teaching, healing, and trying to be accessible to others. Use your time wisely.

June 26

Live in the Moment

Do not allow thoughts to torment you. It is easy to get in this mind set by dwelling on past hurts, sad memories, guilt, and regret. Forgive, forget, and live in the moment for each one is a chance for happiness, don't forfeit it. It has been said about forgiveness that without it the person who will not forgive is likened to someone who has taken poison expecting the other person to die. That is a good analogy. The pleasures of your life should outweigh the pain but that would be in a perfect world. To remain upbeat when you are not in the mood is difficult but, oddly enough, can lift you up. Speak with enthusiasm. You will inspire a confidence you didn't know you had. I often bring someone into your life to do this at the appropriate time, as I know your heart and what will please you.

June 27

I Am Here

Know in your darkest moments I am there. I feel your pain and long to sooth your hurts. Bring them to Me. Leave them as you don't need the baggage. I long to sooth you and bring a peace and joy. Surround yourself with those who you can share your thoughts and feelings. Spend time with people who understand you and can commune with you. There are those out there, but sometimes you need to make the effort to connect. It is a busy world. Often the pace doesn't allow for much fellowship with others. It is important for you to make the time. It will pay off in blessings for both you and the recipient. I promise you this.

June 28

Enjoy Earthly Beauty

Stop, listen to the leaves, the many different sounds of the various trees. Each has a song for you along with the birds that inhabit them. Consider them love songs from Me and gather joy and strength in their beauty. Even shadows can form beautiful patterns if you take the time to look. Shadows are everywhere all through the day and into the evening, ever changing. There for you to enjoy. Each new flower, grass, mushroom, is given to you to explore with your senses at all times of the year and never the same. Contemplate these things of the earth. They are My gifts to you daily. Savor a walk in the woods or your neighborhood. The love I have is shown in these ways until you can be with Me. I am revealed in so many aspects of your life. I am the total of all that is pure and lovely.

June 29

Be Open to Reach Out

If you desire others to reach out to you, sometimes you need to be first. Wait and you will wait a long time. Do not hesitate to call, write, or connect with others as I've given you the means and desire to be involved in the social goings on around you. I work through others. I can bring the needed ingredients into a relationship to foster trust, growth, loyalty, and love. Remain calm and at peace for all will fall into place as I have planned.

June 30

Blessings Await

Do not question My wisdom. I am the keeper of promises. I will not disappoint those who are obedient and care for Me. The pathways are not always smooth, but I am at the end of each new journey. I long to bless you abundantly. Be ready to reap these blessings at the appointed time.

July 1

Mini Breaks to Recharge

I ask that you take mini breaks throughout the day. Do this to contemplate those things you have to be thankful for and commune with Me, the ultimate provider. All must labor in some form. Much of it can be unpleasant. When alternatives are looked at, as in the many negative ways others must survive, your lot can begin to look good. Cherish the joyful, serene, positive times and, when in turmoil, bring them to memory. Even a funny incident can be replayed in your mind to bring a laugh only you can appreciate. I've given you the capacity for this. Use it when needed. I will supply the memory, if you summon Me to do so. You always have available biblical verses that touch you in a special way. These can be an encouragement. It is My living Word to bring life renewed when needed. Don't hesitate to use it when all else fails. It is My love in action.

July 2

Love Dispels Fear

Love conquers fear. Do all with love. Fear will dissipate. When faced with a genuine cause for fear, seek Godly council first. I will come to your aide or connect you with others who will intercede. Stop to contemplate, find time to search within, and I will provide what you need. Too many take on the burden when I promised that *My yoke is easy and My burden light.* So often I want to reprimand *'Oh ye of little faith!' Have I not continually provided in the past?*

July 3

Oasis in the Desert

Yes follow Me. Listen to that still small voice you often ignore. It is for your good that you heed the Holy Spirit, the comforter, the one whom I have provided to bring you closer to Me and what I desire for you. Never despair. The devil takes joy in this. Remain calm in all circumstances. I will provide what is needed. It pleases Me to be of service, the same joy you feel when you reach out to others. See, we are not so different. Remember you were made in the image of Me. Go forth with renewed courage, purpose, and faith. In grace I go before you in all. I will not cause your foot to falter. I am your oasis in the desert.

July 4

Use Your Gifts

I will show you that when you reach out, especially to those I put in your path, a blessing will befall both you and them. It is My purpose to guide You if you'll let Me. You are never as alone as you feel. Your thoughts are not so far afield from those of others. Do you think you are so unique? Yes all are, but share so much as well. Just because you are not experiencing the same emotion as someone else at the moment, doesn't mean they have not shared it at some time in their life. The trials you have been through are not just for your disadvantage but to teach you what to say to others when they need encouragement. Positive words and actions can change lives for the better, just as negative words can bring death and destruction. The tongue, such a small muscle, can be so uplifting or critical. Choose your words carefully with forethought and wisdom. I've given you many gifts. It is up to you to use them.

July 5

I Know the Desires of Your Heart

My arm is not shortened to perform miracles as in the days of Sarah and Abraham. To conceive a child in their old age was unimaginable to them but I knew the desires of their hearts as I do yours. Cling to your faith. Persevere in what I set before you. Patience will bring pleasure in the end but, while I'm preparing you, allow the time for Me to mold you in My image. Ignore the distractions of the world for they bring you further from Me, not closer. Concentrate on what I set before you for you will know what is of value. If you are not sure, spend quiet time in prayer

July 6

I Prepare the Ground

As you grow closer to Me those, who you call friends or family, may distance themselves from you. It is as if you are a foreigner speaking another language. Keep your spirits up for My family, when I was on earth, did not understand My calling even though it was foretold to My mother by an angel before My birth. Those that grew up around Me could not fathom the change in Me when I began to speak of heavenly things. Have patience for they will come around when they are ready. I am preparing the ground as you sow the seed. The time for harvest will come but patience is the key. Do not become discouraged as you are indeed fighting the good fight. Victory is around the corner!

July 7

Avoid Negativity

Those around you are watching. They will begin to understand more as you act in a humble and loving manner. Never underestimate the fact that you are leading even though it seems otherwise. Your good heart and noble intentions cannot be overlooked. They will gain attention in due time. Continue to be an encourager, avoiding negativity at all costs. When things seem most impossible, I stand ready to uphold you. I will further the plans I have for you. Your obedience has not gone unnoticed. It will be rewarded both here on the earth and in heaven.

July 8

Step Forward with Joyful Expectancy

Worry not. Have I not provided for you even in times of hardship? Do not let the joy of the moment be overshadowed by the fears for tomorrow or regrets of yesterday. Everything is being prepared for you. All that is needed is for you to take steps forward toward the blessings I have in store for you. Face each new problem with hope, faith, patience, and expectancy. The belief that all will turn out for the good should be foremost in your thoughts.

July 9

Accepting My Sacrifice Sets Souls Free

All here on earth are spiritual beings in physical bodies. If only they could accept their spirituality and strive to understand it, life would be so much easier. Instead they choose to conform themselves to this world. Its values are ever changing, often involving greed, power, pride, and rebellion. All of the things I hate. True happiness comes from joyful giving, sharing, love, compassion, thankfulness, and a connection with an all loving creator. You were created to fellowship with Me. Remember Adam and Eve? Not much has changed except for My sacrifice. The reality is that it should have changed hearts and minds for the better. In knowing all is forgiven and forgotten, under the blood of Jesus should set all souls free. Instead many are held captive in a labyrinth of Satan's lies. It is sad, but with remedy, if hearts are open to the truth.

July 10

Love Conquers All

Strive for peace, joy, and contentment in your life here on earth until you are reunited with Me. You have in your power all that is needed to live a life of happiness if only you would dwell on the good you can do for others rather than on satisfying only your earthly needs. In reaching out you cause a chain reaction that can nullify negative emotions instantly. 'Love conquers all' is indeed a fact, even with the toughest of opponents. Venture forth with this belief and, I assure you, you will be astounded.

July 11

Peace Beyond Understanding

Rest in Me for I give you a peace that is beyond understanding. Recall a verse, song, or pray a heartfelt prayer, and I will join you. The beauty of today will soon be gone so cherish these few moments with Me. You will be revitalized, refreshed, and renewed. I long to share a few moments with you, so leave time for Me in your busy day.

July 12

Renew Your Spirit

Take mini breaks as the chores of life can be so draining. A few moments of rest, refreshment or exercise can last the whole day in benefits to your mind, spirit, and body. Allow your senses to soak in the wonders of each day, some so brief, others enduring. The sound of a plane passing overhead, the purr of a cat, the ticking of the clock, the songs of birds, and the laughter of children can be a balm to a weary spirit. The soft touch of a loved one, the warmth of a shower, the caress of the wind can renew you and bring such cheer. The smell of a baby, the forest, clean laundry, a delicious meal cooking, momentary pleasures but there for your enjoyment. The colors of a rainbow, sudden flight of a bird, smile of a friend, viewing of a sunrise, all there at one time or another for your pleasure. The sum total of all of your senses and what can be appreciated daily leaves little room for negativity. Revel in beauty and avoid that which tarnishes the mind. It is always your choice, so choose wisely.

July 13

Savor Small Triumphs

Each small triumph in your day brings you closer to your true happiness. As your plan is revealed more clearly strive to make it happen one step at a time. Just as you did as a baby viewing your world with wonderment continue for it all awaits you. Nothing has changed but perhaps your attitude which can be influenced in which ever way you choose. Choose joy. You will experience it.

The affect it has on others will blossom into a tidal wave reaching out beyond what can be seen with the naked eye. You, unfortunately, cannot see all the good that extends to others far beyond an initial act of kindness. I do.

July 14

Seek Me

How can I tell you
how much love I have for you
I can show you in a sunset
in a fireworks display
when you view the distant mountains
or with your children play
If My love could make you happy
it is what I have to give
I can bring it on through others
or give you will to live
There will always be those moments
when life is hard to bear
When you feel you can't go on
and are living in despair
Don't give in to slings and arrows
that the devil throws your way
For you know I live within in you
And am just a prayer away

July 15

Take the First Steps

I ask you to step out in faith. Take those first steps and I will guide you to the next. Your strength to make that move, when the flesh is weak, is a sign of your courage. Don't falter as I am there to catch you. Be confident in your faith. All will fall into place. Be not influenced by those around you. Negative emotions of others will and do affect you. They cause a veil of sorrow and discontent if not put in check. Be steadfast in following Me and My teachings being obedient, humble, and devout. The rest will follow.

July 16

You Were Made For Action

Walk with Me, literally. Go outside and commune with Me as you take in all that is around you. Your physical movement is vital to the upkeep of your body. Don't neglect it as it will affect your health and happiness. You were made for action and lack of it will only make you listless and strip you of energy. Listen to the sounds of nature. Enjoy the smells and sights around you. The smallest weed breaking through a crack in the sidewalk can teach you a lesson of perseverance.

July 17

I See and Am Pleased

Care for those I send to you. This includes children, animals, friends, loved ones, and sometimes others I put in your path. You have so much to give and your sacrifices will be rewarded. You forget how much you have already done but it has only enriched others in ways you may never know. Be pleased with what I am saying. Gain confidence for I am commending you for your faithfulness and loyalty to Me and Mine.

July 18

Negative Self Talk

Self talk can be so damaging yet it can be present without your immediate awareness. Eradicate it as soon as you notice it. Replace it with thankfulness and praise to Me. You will see it, as quickly, disappear for evil cannot abide in My presence. Remember this with each breath. All will be well.

July 19

One Step at a Time

Take time to do all that is needed. Do not rush or limit the time you give to those jobs you do. When you hurry you cannot do your best. It is in hurrying that accidents occur. I can help you to slow down. You need only ask. There is time to do all you need to do. I will not allow you to become overwhelmed. I will help you to make those lists or tackle those jobs one step at a time. It helps not to look at the whole picture but take baby steps. Life is a puzzle. You and I can put the pieces together to make a masterpiece. You'll see.

July 20

Know Victory is Yours

Take heed in looking ahead or behind but look to the moment. Things never are or were totally the way you remember or imagine they will be. You tend to gloss over times you pictured as ideal when in reality you struggled then as now. You are and never were alone as you envisioned, for others have experienced the same challenges, frustrations, and losses as you have, just in a different setting. They also face the same fears and obstacles as well just as you have and will. Take heart and go forth with renewed courage. As a child of Mine, you will experience victory. Relish this fact. Remember I am faithful to fulfill all My promises.

July 21

Life's Music

Life is a song with many melodies. They range in tempo and beat with subtle messages conveyed in life's lessons. What would life be without its music? The song of a bird, the cry of a child, the joy in laughter, the whoosh of the waves, and the crunch of autumn leaves are just some parts of this marvelous symphony. Enjoy the music while it lasts for a heavenly choir awaits for your enjoyment more powerful than your wildest imaginings.

July 22

You Can Lean on Me

Wait on the Lord; be of good courage, and He shall strengthen your heart; Wait, I say on the Lord. Psalm 27:14

Yes, your patience will be rewarded. Take heart that I hear and understand your longings and the deepest desires of your heart. I have and will fulfill your needs as they arise without your asking. What more can you hope for then to have Me to lean on?

July 23

Cast Discouraging Thoughts Away

Do not be troubled or weary. Cast those fears, worries, and regrets away as I can renew your spirit with the living water I promised upon My departure from this earth. Just ask with belief and faith that I will restore you. It will come to pass before you know it.
I will raise you up on eagle's wings to soar above the earthly woes and sorrows you have experienced. Just as there will be no more tears in heaven, I can dry those tears on earth as well. I replace them with gladness and new hope. All is within your grasp. Reach out in faith and claim it.

July 24

Trust in Me

I will bring all of your works to completion if you trust in Me. I know the tasks before you. I can lighten your load while leading you in the right direction. No duty is too difficult for Me. I will guide you in all you do and provide the wisdom when you but ask for it. Do not expect to carry each burden alone for that is just what defeats you. Why refuse help when it is so freely and gladly offered?

July 25

Your Choice

I've told you that with Me your burdens will be light. Can you not see this already coming to pass in subtle ways? Do not doubt My promises for, with Me, you are guaranteed success. Be obedient to look to Me for guidance in all you do. I will not forsake you. As for leaving you, there is no chance. For I have always remained faithful to you even when you have been absent from Me. You can always come home to Me for I leave the door wide open. It is you who must step through it.

July 26

The Depth of My Love

I know the depth of your love. It cannot touch the depth of Mine. You will know this more fully someday. You will glorify Me the more for it. I wish you could feel it more fully than you do right now. As your desire becomes deeper you will reach a higher level of intimacy. It is for this you should strive. You will not be disappointed.

July 27

Rest in My Peace

And I said, "Oh, that I had wings like a dove! For then I would fly away and be at rest. Psalm 55:6

Oh that I could scoop you up into My arms and carry you into My bosom to hold and comfort you in those times of struggle and hardship. If you could see that is exactly what I am doing as I am strengthening you in these trials. Take comfort in My words to you that I am ready always to be your shield and your protector through every storm of life. Call out to Me. I am there instantly for you are cherished beyond measure, My beloved. Glory in that. Rest in the peace I bring.

July 28

Safeguard Your Earthly Temple

I will bring to completion the works you do for Me. As you can already see I am being faithful to you as you have been to Me. Do not let discouragement take hold for it is easy in this earthly realm. That is what My precious people fight against daily as the enemy uses this tool of his with delight to cause dissatisfaction, depression, strife, and hardship. When you are in its grip, the tormentor uses it to take you further from My kingdom. My desire is for your joy here on earth until you meet with Me in heaven. It is attainable but can be intercepted when this spirit of torment enters an earthly soul. Guard against it with the word of God, a powerful mighty sword against the enemy. As I have said, he cannot dwell in My midst. Use the tools I have given you which are your strong faith, My word, prayer, and fellowship with others of like mind. Guard your spirit, mind, and body. It is your earthly temple, the temporary home of your heavenly spirit. It is your precious possession, given by Me, to safeguard at all cost.

July 29

Joy is Attainable

Do not sorrow, for the joy of the Lord is your strength. Nehemiah 8:10

This joy is attainable and sustainable in a closer relationship with Me. You have felt it at various times of your life and have been lifted up. It is there for you when you whole heartedly desire it. Strive for this. It is My heart's longing to satisfy this need in My people above all else.

July 30

Full Armor of God

You are attaining your goal as you strive to please Me. There is more to come with richness and blessings untold. I am pleased with your obedience and ask that you hold fast to your faith. Guard against the snares of the devil for his deviousness cannot be overemphasized. You have been held captive before in the traps he has set for you. Be leery of his evil mighty presence in this his earthly realm. His workers, in the spirit, roam the earth looking for whom they can torment. Guard your body, your earthly temple, with the full armor of God. Daily guard yourself by putting on the full armor of God. (See Ephesians; 6: 10-20)

July 31

You are My Hands and Feet

I have given you the knowledge of how to protect yourself, commune with Me, and reach out to others. You are My hands and feet, the only tools you need on earth have been given you. Use them wisely, seeking My council when you are in doubt. I am always near and a breath away when My beloved children call. Hold fast to your faith for it will sustain you in the storms of life and during life's celebrations.

August 1

My Word Divinely Inspired

Heed not what the highly esteemed 'scholars' say about the holy Bible that is negative. It is a work that has been translated repeatedly, however, it nevertheless remains divinely inspired. I still reign from the heavens above. I have dominion over man whom I have created. All who took part in that holy undertaking were under great obligation to get it right. Not a comma is out of place. The hope and wisdom it has given throughout the ages has been My well of living water to thirsty souls world wide. Do not believe the ramblings of the so called scholars, for they will have to answer to Me. Will they ever be surprised and enlightened in the end.

August 2

Freedom Comes at a Cost

So many die who seek democracy under wicked rulers the world over. It is only natural to desire the freedoms required to live an enjoyable life. More are risking all to make a statement. Their courage and determination will win out in the end but, sadly, many must suffer and some die to set things right. It is this same determination of My followers who are being persecuted world wide to bring goodness and understanding to a hurting world. Those who listen and heed will be rewarded.

August 3

Look to the Rainbow

Those we love most can hurt us the deepest. It is a true fact and yet with faith you can endure even this. Stay connected to others who can comfort you. All have experienced rejection at one time or another and survived to become stronger. You will as well. I have equipped you with the ability to meet this and other struggles ahead. Do not be downhearted. Grasp the hope I set before you like a rainbow, ever a delight after a storm.

August 4

Partake of My Love and Grace

How many of My own have lost their way to become prisoners of a greedy, hectic, secular world? Never stopping to enjoy even the smallest pleasures but reaching for the unreachable. When will they realize all of this grasping yields nothing but dissatisfaction. My ways will meet their needs without the pain they are up against seeking their own fulfillment. If they would but seek My face all would be much simpler and satisfying. The despair that they feel I mirror yet am helpless to correct unless they reach out. Free will can hinder or cause new beginnings. It can also unleash pride and rebellion, two qualities I abhor. In humbleness and supplication I can work My miracles, but evil cannot exist in My presence. My ever present love endures. I long for all to partake.

August 5

Holy Spirit Yours for the Asking

To those who follow Me I give the Holy Spirit, the comforter to bring solace in times of trouble, grace to bear all. It was and is My promise from days gone by when My spirit was reunited with My Father following My death upon the cross. When the curtain in the temple was rend in two, so was a new era born. One in which offerings no longer needed to be made, but I, the ultimate offering, brought forgiveness to all who sought it. With that also came the promise of the Comforter, to dwell within those who seek My presence.

August 6

I Will Provide

Take all in life with gratitude and joy for each day brings new blessings to be acknowledged and delighted in. You are My precious children in whom I am well pleased. Take pleasure in this as I know your struggles. I try to keep the trials at bay amidst your daily tasks. Marvel in how smoothly most days go. Meet the challenges you face with a renewed hope that I will shore you up when needed. Am I not providing as promised? Dispel those fears for, do I not provide for the smallest of My creations as well as the large in a simple logical manner? Look around you and be reassured of My care for you.

August 7

You are Never Alone

It is after you have been with others that you might feel the most lonely. You were made to be social, to commune with others. So many lament their moments in solitude, however even then you are not totally alone. It is I who dwells within those who have accepted Me, so they are never truly alone. Remember this and find joy in the quiet moments as well as the busy ones with others. Share that quiet time with Me. I long for your company and conversation. Speak aloud to Me for I hear you and I will answer, even in just a small gentle voice. You will feel My presence. Loneliness comes only when you forget about the One who is always with you.

August 8

My Warm Embrace

The warmth you feel upon your shoulders is not only of the sun. It is My gentle caress of contentment. You are experiencing My love enfolding you without your knowledge. Someday this will be common place, a joy immeasurable. A day in the near future when all will become as a fog passing to bring clarity and understanding. Cherish those remembered moments for I am giving you a glimpse of paradise, your heavenly reward for holding on to your faith and understanding and being obedient. Yes, there is a crown and a new name for you in heaven that will set you apart as Mine.

August 9

Keep Today Separate from Tomorrow

Do not give tomorrow your time today. In this you steal today's joy. Bring to mind only the immediate moment's beauty for, how can you fully enjoy one thing when contaminated with another? Live for the moment for, the moment will never return in quite the same way. My joy is in your happiness. Experience it to the fullest with My blessings and love.

August 10

Change My Mindset

Yes, I can give you a new mindset if you ask Me. Do not let your life become routine, ever. Vary each day's experiences knowingly so that I can bring new joys your way. When you get in the routine rut, it can cause you to be downcast without knowing why. Have a giving heart, bringing smiles and happiness to others. This will be as a mirror reflecting these same joys back to you. Try it. I will help you make it happen. You've seen the pleasure you have when you are a blessing to others through your giving of encouraging words or specially chosen gifts. It is My joy to give back to you the wondrous feeling you experience.

August 11

Your Faith has Set You Free

When I told Moses to tell the people My name is 'I am' it signified that among all names, I reign supreme. When I said *I am the father of Abraham, Isaac and Jacob*, although they are dead in body, they still exist as will you at the end of your life. Is this so hard to fathom? Believe and live as though forever for you inherit an eternity through My sacrifice and your accepting of Me as the one true God. Hold fast to your hope in Me for it will get you through the hardest of times. My promises I will and have fulfilled throughout history. Cling to Me as you would a life preserver as, that is what I am to those who follow Me. To those who are perishing all of this is nonsense.

August 12

Faithful Prayers Release Power From Above

My angels watch over you and yours because of your faithfulness and prayers. Protection does not come cheap even in the spiritual world. When you pray the full armor of God over yourself and loved ones you permit the angels to go forth against the evil spirits dwelling in the earthly realm. A hedge of protection surrounds them to keep them safe when you are not able to intervene. When you place them in My hand, evil has no recourse but to flee. Good and evil are like two ends of magnetic poles repelling each other. The one cannot overtake the other. Goodness and love are potent enemies of evil and darkness. Darkness has no choice but to flee. Seek only to be in the light. Be My candle out in the world and picture yourself as such for it is as a ripple in a pond spreading ever outward to those who need it most. As hearts are drawn to Me My purpose is revealed and lives are made new. To be a part of this is a great honor and you will know I smile upon you.

August 13

Small Acts of Encouragement Bring Joy

Seek to uplift others in all you do. The burdens faced by them are often unknown but enough to cause deep pain. A kind word or smile can sometimes work small miracles. Look at all who followed Me in the hope I would bring freedom, peace, and comfort in their turbulent world. You can carry a small portion of this through your encouragement which in turn gets passed on to others. Small waves often join the larger ones to cause a tidal wave of joy.

August 14

Open Your Heart

Take time to notice others and speak with them whenever possible. Rushing through life takes away from many small pleasures. It gets you no further ahead. Be mindful of those around you. It takes but a few minutes to show Godly love and concern. No one will put blame on you for caring. It's ignoring the needs of those in your midst that steals your blessing and theirs. Open your heart to others and you will be fulfilled.

August 15

Reach Out

Your love can move mountains and conquer evil. Explore the endless possibilities of reaching out in new ways. There are hot lines, hospitals, nursing homes, food kitchens, needy children to sponsor in distant lands, clean drinking water to provide, and so many other ways of reaching others that the list is endless. The needs are great, not only physical but spiritual as well. Satisfy the physical. That opens the door to the spiritual realm. Reaching out can only draw others to you as evidenced by My life on earth.

August 16

Heartfelt Prayer

A simple heartfelt prayer can bring such miraculous results. Often those simple prayers are forgotten. When I answer them you are not aware and miss a blessing. You ask how can so many live in poverty, hunger, destitution, and squalor? Injustice is a part of this life for some. In the aspect of eternity, this short time on earth matters little. The way others interact with My needy shows service to Me. It also proves that hearts turned outward to others reap the most benefits. Service unto Me, through those who are deserving, is the highest act here on earth in which to gain favor.

August 17

Hold Fast to Your Faith.

I have gone to prepare a place for you as it is written. Be expectant. It will astound and satisfy you for I know the desires of your heart. I am the keeper of promises. Even My rainbow is a reminder of this. Hold fast to your faith. It will sustain you though life's battles until you can come home.

August 18

The More You Give

The more you give, it will be given back to you in greater measure. You have and will see this more as you dive into service to others. Examples can be seen in all facets of your life. The joy you feel is a result of what you are doing. Don't be surprised when your cup is filled to overflowing time and again.

August 19

Much Greater Things

As I said much greater things will be done on earth than I have done through the Holy Spirit whom I left as a comforter, source of strength, and healer. The time is coming for testing and proving My promises true. Be bold in your faith as, by putting it into action, it will bring honor to My name and draw others closer to Me.

August 20

Heed My Voice

Dissatisfaction with life, job, or other aspects of existence is common when you are not accomplishing what you believe needs to be done. It can be frustrating. Do not become discouraged as I often work on the sidelines setting situations in motion. What you see with earthly eyes is often not what I have intended. Be patient and do not try to hurry in bringing your plans (My) to fruition. I frequently have a better way to bring the results you desire. Seek Me in prayer asking for direction and when it seems I do not answer, it is not the appointed time for action. Heed My voice for, when you can discern it, you have reached a higher level of spirituality. Strive for this as I desire a closer intimacy with you as well.

August 21

Reach Out to Others

Reach out as you have been doing to others. I am opening doors for further opportunities to minister. Your willingness to be open, honest, and welcoming will draw those who are in need to you. Through you I can do what needs to be accomplished. Shine your light so that others may be illuminated. I will make your paths straight.

August 22

I Am in Control

Yes, I control it all. Be forewarned that you cannot know My power until you are in its presence. Let it sweep over you for with it you, as well, can know victory. No circumstance is ever quite the same. I am the master of surprises, miracles, and wonders. Never lose the awe and sense of wonder you possess. Dare to cling to your dreams, hopes, and faith for a future of work for Me. In it you will be the apple of My eye while working along side Me. We are partners equal in value when moving in the Spirit. The blessings I've been pouring out are but a mere pittance when compared with the vast array in store for all who hold Me on high. Your praises do not go unheeded. My precious one, I keep you under My wing.

August 23

Seek Me in Prayer

As you go forth in love, service, and obedience a new world will open up. One with different assignments daily to bring renewal, hope, and purpose where there seemed to be none. Do not look at time in quite the same way. I will provide the opportunities, even in your busy day. Remember to exercise, both physically and spiritually, keeping your body fit to meet the challenges I am allowing you to face while learning more and more of Me. I put before you the people and resources to bring you further in your walk. As you are learning to discern My voice, it seems as ideas are flowing faster than you can take them in. Go forth with caution. Test and think out each step by using the knowledge gained through others. Read more of what I have been placing before you. The choices you make should be more reverent now, seeking Me in prayer to affirm that your path is the correct one leading you to further service for My kingdom. Ultimately, a closer relationship with Me is developing in increments. You will begin to experience exceeding joy. You have only just put your toes in the water of what is in store. Be faithful and tenacious. All will fall into place as you and I desire.

August 24

My Chosen Vessel

Chosen vessels are what I call My elected ones. You choose to use the gifts I've filled you with to go forth in service to Me. In holy reverence you spread joy, peace, kindness, and wisdom to those in need. As you learn more of Me and what I expect, your ministry will open up into a larger more fulfilling one. Your patience these many years is beginning to reap rewards that touch others in ways you cannot see. Be faithful, taking each step in its own time. I will bring to pass all that you desire and more.

August 25

Avoid Worry

You are right to discourage others from worrying. So much pleasure is lost in worry about what will never happen. Enjoy each moment for they are precious and fleeting. View each new day as another adventure so different from any other and offering so many opportunities for you to be a blessing.

August 26

Tears Begin the Healing

Just as the rain cleanses the environment, tears remove the hurt and begin the healing. How would you ever know true happiness if you had not experienced some trials, sorrows, and hardships? You are being molded like a fine piece of art, a rare statue unique and special. All that has occurred in your life has made you what you are. Cherish your experiences both positive and negative for, through them, you have been made stronger and more confident.

August 27

Avoid Negative Self Talk

Self talk can be negative. Action and service are antidotes to this. You are bombarded with messages in this fast paced world. Your brain becomes acclimated to this and often takes over when understimulated. Purge negative thoughts with pure ones. Seek an uplifting church, the Bible, service to others or any positive activity. It can be as simple as a walk in the woods. I am here to sooth you but sometimes it is up to you to act first.

August 28

Another Sense

I have given you more than the five senses you are aware of. Intuition is another that you don't consider, but which comes in handy when you are about to make important choices. When you are able to sense another's hurt or the general mood in an environment you have just entered, you are experiencing discernment which is the realm of the Holy Spirit. As you grow it becomes stronger and more accurate. Use it wisely. It is My gift to you.

August 29

Be Faithful to Gather Together

Do not forsake the gathering together of those who freely talk of Me. When you do I am in your midst. Isn't that exciting? Your corporate prayers are powerful. They never go unheard. I answer them in My own way in My own time. Do not doubt this. The possibilities are endless in how I can turn things around for the good. I am an expert at it. Look at the Red sea, only one example of a past miracle. The extra effort made to go to a Bible study or prayer group always brings blessings. With these efforts I am well pleased.

August 30

Your Reverence Will be Rewarded

Who is qualified to know the mind of God? My ways are not your ways and often, when brought to their knees, My people who listen to My voice are given the desires of their hearts. Do not feel betrayed when things do not turn out as you believe they will for a far greater blessing will befall those who have been obedient, seek My face, and do not falter in their walk with Me. My plans are far deeper and more complicated then can be imagined by mere mortals. Death can be a release but also open other doors that have remained closed due to unbelief. Death can be life to those who come to Me with a humble heart for the rewards are not often visible through earthly eyes. Stand firm in the unity of each other together with a common purpose. Your reverence will be rewarded a thousand fold.

August 31

Memories to Cherish

I often bring to you those who are in need, be they humans or pets. You are their caretakers, and though they are dependent upon you, you reap the benefits through your service and care. Being in the company of these others brings its own rewards in laughter, love, and play. Make the time to spend with them for the benefits are in the sharing of these special times together. Moments of memories are to be cherished when the absence of their presence becomes a reality. Create those mind pictures to treasure always, for they will not fade as do earthly possessions.

September 1

Enjoy the Ride

As your life unfolds it is as if you have lived many mini existences. These all add up to the person you have become but, when looked back upon, seem like other lifetimes. During these changes, barely noticed by you as time goes by, it is as if you are a combination of different people at various intervals. Where did that time go and who was I back then that I should be as I am today you might ask? Change happens as we greet each new day be it grown children, completed schooling, a move to a different local, or an illness in our own or immediate family. Sometimes it can be a tragedy such as a fire, car accident or death which may happen in either of the former events as well. How did we ever survive all that we have been through we may ask? But in it all I have been with you helping you to weather whatever burdens had to be endured. No amount of preplanning could have prepared you for your journey. Relax, enjoy the ride, for I will be with you through it all. Just hold My hand. Let Me guide you. It is My pleasure to do so.

September 2

Small Acts Reap Big Rewards

Small acts can bring the greatest rewards to those who value them. Never hesitate to make a call, send a note, invite someone to your home or make a visit. If I bring someone to mind, it is often because I want you to pray for them. In so doing I may then ask you to visit, call, write a letter or email, or perform some duty you may question. You will know it is of Me if it is a kindness. In acting on My prompting you will bless yourself far more then the one you've reached out to. Make the time, even when the thought to do any of these things seems an effort. I will provide the energy

September 3

Be Mindful of Your Dreams

Do not discount dreams as ways I can reach you and get a message across. Even though a dream may seem silly or confusing, think out what I am showing you for clues to the message. If more people would heed their dreams and seek divine guidance in interpreting them, they would be better prepared for times to come. As in the past, I have used dreams to help prepare and explain present and future events.

September 4

Dreary Days

Do not allow a dreary day to dampen your spirits. Be uplifted by joyous thoughts and happy remembrances. Let the sun shine inward on those days for your countenance will glow and bring cheer to others. Stay active to keep your spirits up for it is when you forgo activity that depression can set in. Do not let it get a foothold. For many it can be debilitating. There is much to be thankful for. Let your gratefulness for it all be uplifting to your mind, body, and spirit.

September 5

Curb a Loose Tongue

Careless remarks are just that. Those who utter them are often unaware of the pain or discomfort they cause. All spoken should be well thought out as some of the worst outcomes are begun by a loose tongue. But the good that can be delivered to others in the form of praise, kindness, and love cannot be overstated. This far outweighs any evil in this world. Seek out those who are encouraging, wise, and caring for they will inspire the best in you. Aspire for a virtuous, giving heart and your efforts will be rewarded.

September 6

Keep a Positive Attitude

Listen to the music of the leaves in the trees, the wind as it blows, the crashing ocean waves, the songs of birds, crickets, and frogs among other things. It is a worldly serenade especially for you. Enjoy the peace and joy these small pleasures bring. They help to fortify you for more difficult times. They bring peace to a troubled spirit in their remembrance. Difficulties seem to over ride all the good out there so be mindful that '*this too will pass.*' The positive always far out weighs the negative. It is easy for you to allow trials to swallow you up in worry and lament. Keep it all in Godly perspective. Know that you are in the palm of My hand, well protected, and loved.

September 7

Seek a Cheerful Countenance

A glad heart is indeed a treasure. It is easy for a melancholy mood to snatch up happiness. Be aware of how quickly this can happen. Keep your thoughts in check. Do you know that most of the negative thoughts you have about yourself are untrue. The worries that can plague you rob you of precious moments of happiness. Remember an uplifting quote or scripture verse at times like this. Grasp the hope it brings for it is a joyous journey I wish for you until you reach your heavenly home.

September 8

You are Protected

I keep watch over you even when you sleep. As a mother or father tends their children until they are safely in bed, My love for you is your cover. Doubt not that you are greatly loved and protected under My wings. Find peace and hope in this as you begin each day anew.

September 9

Further Protection

Behavior can be greatly influenced by negative spirits taking control of a human of any age. To see this is unnerving especially in the spirit when there is such a decided contrast. Stand firm in your faith with the knowledge that in My name these spirits must come under submission. Let your holy boldness control any situation as you consult Me in prayer for wisdom and protection. Cover yourself daily and others with the full armor of God as is emphasized in Ephesians chapter 6. Your ministering angels will do the rest with a shout of 'allelulua!' they go forth in My name.

September 10

Embrace Positive Thoughts

As you go about your day pray unceasingly. The world that you inhabit is but for a brief time. You are of a spirit nature. You are related to that realm more closely than this one. For this reason you will be most satisfied when you dwell on heavenly things. Do not let the troubles of earth bring you down for, negative thinking colors all that you do. Avoid it at all costs dwelling on happy thoughts, memories, and the things in life that have brought laughter and joy. This will sustain you through the tough times that are an inevitable part of life. You are cherished as a unique creation. You bring blessings to others in more ways than you know. Be encouraged by this. Know that under My watchful eyes you are protected.

September 11

Free Choice Allows Evil

It is so hard to grasp the evil that can dwell in this world. All are created with free will. Those that choose the right paths bring glory to My name. I weep for the devastation that can be unleashed by those that make the wrong choices. They face the terrible consequences along with their unfortunate victims. In their paths I have placed many who have tried to influence them in positive ways but the choice is still theirs in the end. When this happens I try to turn even those situations around for My glory by comforting those affected through the presence of the Holy Spirit and the works of others in their lives. A song, written or spoken words, a gesture, or scene in nature can often minister to these hurting hearts in such a way to bring healing. I always make a way to show My constant love.

September 12

My Blessing for You

If you desire a closer walk with Me try these exercises for a week. I will meet you where you are if you reach out in the ways I'll explain. First, read My living word, the Bible for twenty minutes. This inspired word is needed for instruction, reproof, rebuke, but most of all to demonstrate My love in words that can only deepen your relationship with Me. I can speak to you through these words as they are powerful and full of life. Take another twenty minutes to pray using the acronym ACTS to fully approach prayer in all its attributes. When you seek Me with adoration, confession, thanksgiving, and supplication, I can appreciate all you are to Me and as a loving father shower you with My blessings. Lastly, and the hardest of all, is to wait quietly for a minimum of twenty minutes to hear from Me. Make sure you are devoid of distractions to make the most of this time in which I can commune with you. One hour is all I ask you give me broken down into Bible reading (*study to find yourselves approved*), prayer, and introspection. You will feel My presence during this, our time. Don't hesitate to give yourself this blessing I long to share with you.

September 13

My Treasure

Just as you would search for a treasure glistening in the sun, I look at you as My treasure, unique so gifted but often not knowing this and needing My reassurance. I long for you to fulfill My plan but the world interferes at every turn. Just as the flesh interrupts My work with its demands, others are pulling you in all directions through guilt and obligations. When you make time for Me, you will always be rewarded. Try it and see. Have patience. I will reveal My plan for your life. In this you will be fulfilled.

September 14

I Have Brought You This Far

I surround you with all that is needed. Reach out and grasp that which is within your reach. My hand is not shortened when it comes to bestowing blessings on My own. Persevere and you will be rewarded beyond your broadest speculations. Look at from whence you've come and make comparisons. You will be amazed at the prayers you have prayed that have been answered. Do not dwell on those unanswered as ultimately they would not have fulfilled your destination, barring your path to complete your heavenly plan. I provide it, but you must be willing, obedient, and listen for My voice. Make that quiet time. You will know what I mean. The steps of a righteous man are ordered. My promises are ripe to be granted.

September 15

Allow Me to Uphold You

Allow Me to carry you in your times of weakness and stress. As you grow weary from the burdens of life, I long to shore you up, strengthen, and protect you under My wing. Doubt not what I have in store for you. Do not press your physical body beyond its limitations. Just remember tomorrow is another day. I can easily refresh those who need My living water. Taste and your thirst will be quenched. Attend church for there your spirit will be renewed for a new work week. My Holy Spirit can recharge your batteries, giving a fresh infilling of power to your weary body, mind, and soul. Neglect not this resource. If your current church does not leave you feeling changed in a positive way when you depart, seek My will in finding another more to your satisfaction.

September 16

A Glimpse of What Awaits

Heaven is a glorious place of bright sunshine never a shadow or a dismal day. Imagine each day like this in which to delight in only beauty, goodness, and joy. Tearful reunions with those so dear await you as well as new acquaintances with those of old including My prophets, apostles, mother, father, and others spoken of in the Bible. This is but a mere glimpse of what is to come. We will be together never to be separated, our spirits melded, mended, and glorified. To sing with the angels new songs and those of old making music with heavenly instruments. Your mansion awaits to your specifications. Be patient and hold the course for you will, indeed, be rewarded for your faithfulness, My beloved.

September 17

Spend Time With Me

It is all I ask that you spend time with Me to listen to My voice and commune with Me. Is it so much to ask in the busy whirl of your life that you, the apple of My eye and object of My love, show Me a little attention? For it is at these times that I can lavish My love upon you and speak of the blessings I have in store for you. When you give Me this chance, you are the benefactor. There is so much to do. Time is growing short. Be My hands and feet for My loved ones need ministering to. Sometimes it is only that human contact that can make a difference, a physical reaching out in word and deed. Perhaps it is only a needed hug. Go forth in service for Me. You will be richly rewarded.

September 18

Seek Godly Wisdom

You can mold those around you into what I want them to be. Some have a talent for this but it can be developed over time. Seek wisdom, My Godly wisdom. Don't hesitate to ask for it as I will grant your request. Each task you face should be approached with courage and the belief of accomplishment through Me. The challenges of life are there to be met to strengthen you but also to encourage others through your shared experiences.

September 19

Be Doers of the Word

It is not enough to merely acknowledge that I am real and so too the truth of all that is written in My Holy word, the Bible. You must be doers of the word, that is, step out in faith to walk in My footsteps in a hurting world. To minister to others as I did while on earth is the highest of accomplishments you could ever ask for. I am and always will be right beside you so hesitate not but go forth with holy boldness. I will lead the way, set your path, and help to bring light and joy where there is desolation and despair. With your hand in Mine we can do anything. Never doubt this. You must believe with all your heart that I am in this with you to the finish. Press on and never give in to despair or become overwhelmed with life's challenges. These are the devil's greatest tools.

September 20

Sleepless Nights and Dreams

Those sleepless nights are sometimes the only time I can get your attention. Do not ignore My beckoning. It is often hard to get your attention during your busy day, but when you are at rest I can whisper My words in your ear. It is those who listen who reap the rewards. Be mindful of your dreams as well for there are lessons to be learned and events to be foreshadowed. Heed your dreams for I speak to you through those as well for knowledge and to help you prepare for what is to come.

September 21

Our Spiritual Link

Heavenly songs await you but earthly songs sustain you now. The music of the earth is trivial in comparison to what is to come. Yet you delight in it all, the bird's song, the ocean's roar, the gentle purr of a cat, the warning bark of a dog, the laughter of all especially children. This is what makes you divinely human here upon the earth. I smile at your joy and delight. I share each of your sorrows for we have a spiritual link that cannot be broken when you choose to follow Me. The heavens rejoice when that choice is made, for evil cannot exist when goodness is embraced.

September 22

Don't Miss the Opportunity

The journey of life seems long but it is a mere blink in eternity. So many miss the beauty of a relationship with Me on earth, when it is so easy, tangible, and within their reach. I offer many chances to choose Me, but so many turn away losing a relationship that could only strengthen them and fortify them in a world that offers many challenges. Together we can meet them. If they only knew I am only a prayer away, so easy yet unattainable for many. You were created for shared pleasure, Me with you, but also to fellowship with others in My name. So often this divine plan has gone wrong through strict religious dogma, misunderstandings, and human disputes. Loving Me should be easy and a pleasure, not a hardship as so many make it out to be. I say give Me a try and if it doesn't work, won't you be the first one to know? You may be pleasantly surprised.

September 23

A Soul Experience

How can I prove My everlasting presence? For those who believe without proof, I am so touched for you see the world and all its splendor as My handiwork. Draw near to Me through, prayer, worship, songs, and your quiet time and I will inhabit that space. You will feel My tangible presence and My holy spirit will affirm it to you as a soul experience. Bask in this love I so freely offer.

September 24

Go Forth With a Cheerful Heart

My work should never be a chore, but taken up with a glad and willing heart. For, in that spirit, you will be a light to a world so filled with darkness. If only they would come to Me to find solace, grace, forgiveness, and joy, I would so fill them that they would never thirst again for the things of this world. Oh, that I could open their blind eyes to what I can provide. It often takes a nudge from an outside source such as you to be as a key to the lock freeing their spirits to look to Me as their comforter. Be bold and courageous in seeking them out for I will give you a peace in all of these undertakings.

September 25

A Fresh Start

Each new day can bring a fresh start. When viewed this way, yesterday's burdens can be discarded like trash. The sadness, worry, and torment excised from your mind. I can help you with this through prayer and the belief that all is in My hands to take care of in My own way. The tears of yesterday I've dried. The pain and sorrow I've carried with you. My gentle embrace will give you the courage to face another day. Believe in your ability to face all with Me steadfastly beside you. You will, indeed, be a conqueror.

September 26

What of Value do You Long For?

Share what you've learned of Me with others. They are weary for news from home, their heavenly home that is. From whence do they think they originate? This is not their true dwelling place. It will suffice for now but their longings are not for the material things of this world that wear out and fade away. That is why when procured these things do not bring satisfaction. Then is sought other entertainments, mood elevators, and gadgets to fill that hole which cannot be satiated. It is Me that they truly seek. Will they ever learn or go on endlessly rejecting Me until it is too late?

September 27

You Will Never Grow Old

Never lose your sense of wonder or your ability to dream of plans to fulfill. All humans are uniquely different, so desires vary. An artist's quest to portray his thoughts on paper will vastly differ from a mountain climber who seeks the highest peak. As long as you have aspirations, you will never grow old in the sense of a purpose for your life. While there is still breath in you, your greatest challenge will be to lead others to Me. But I am there to help you reach that saintly goal. The trumpets of heaven will sound with the return of its prodigals. They will then know the depths of their Father's love.

September 28

I Will Bear Your Pain With You

In your darkest moments, I wait with open arms. The sadness and sorrows of this world are inevitable. With love comes heartache. I'll bear the pain with you. You will feel My presence in a glorious sunrise or the birth of a baby. The wonders of this world far outweigh its evils. Dwell on happy thoughts, fond memories, and a heaven to come.

September 29

Free Will Choose Wisely

When I gave free will to Adam and Eve, they had everything their hearts could desire including the chance to walk in the Garden of Eden, a paradise beyond measure. Just as you have free choice as well to choose good over evil, do not suffer their fate. To be separated from Me was the ultimate punishment they would have to endure. Life could no longer be carefree, easy, and peaceful without the woes presented to the human race daily. That is why free choice is still an option. Could I ever force My precious ones to choose Me knowing that they did not do it willingly? Just as your betrothed could not approach you under gun point and declare, "You better marry Me or else." What kind of a relationship would that be? I present choices throughout your lifetime, chances to change direction if need be through gentle nudges. Sometimes these are not so gentle. Have you found your relationship with Me a burden? Your story and others are a testimony to My gentle loving kindness offering grace to all even the worst of sinners. Forgiveness is only a heart's cry away, yet so few take this step. If only they knew the joy available by choosing Me, a life of hardship could be avoided. So many grasp that thread of independence, rebelliousness, and pride, which, in the end, is their downfall. In choosing Me, there will still be times of trouble in this lifetime. In clinging to My hand all is made so much less of a struggle. Heed these words for I only ever speak in truth, My beloved, to encourage, enlighten, and fulfill. My love for you is endless. I long to pour it out upon you like a fine anointing oil, bestowing abundant blessings upon your life to bring you new joy and hope.

September 30

A Loving Family

Next to Me, cherish family above all else for the blood link you share is the embodiment of happiness. Avoid hurtful words and criticism for, the closer the bond, the deeper the hurt. I endorse the family and what it stands for. Value kindness, goodwill, nurturing, and the love that binds you together. You will find in your life many types or models of family be it in your work, church, school, neighborhood or town. These are the smaller units that circle the inner most one which is family. The others surround like the planets encircle the sun, each with their own agendas. Those family units are exemplified by your actual family, your work family, your friends and neighbors, and your church family. My greatest desire is that all on the earth would look to Me as the head of the family, following the commandments I set out to live by in peace and harmony until we can all be united in heaven. No more wars, famines, divorce, disease, or natural disasters but an earth to model after the Garden of Eden. Here we can share fellowship with each other until physical death and resurrection where you will dwell forever with Me in heaven. Your mansion awaits. It is built to your specifications for I know the desires of your heart. I long to please you.

October 1

A Joyful Reunion

So many live in fear of death. I've made the transition easy, like stepping from one room into another. Just as birth is an effortless arrival into this world, your exit is accomplished in much the same way amidst rejoicing. You are welcome in the familiar place from which you came. Your triumphant ascension brings the epitome of joy, the opposite of the reaction of those who are on earth. Their time will come. Celebrations are more the order of what should really be happening here on earth. If they only knew. Their sadness will someday be replaced in heaven by jubilant rejoicing and a home coming to rival any event however carefully prepared on earth. My loving arms await My earthly disciples.

October 2

Fear Not the Death of Body but of Soul

You learn your craft more thoroughly each day through trial and error. There are some who never learn from their mistakes. Their journey is made so much longer by not paying attention to the lessons I am teaching. Often drugs or alcohol stand in the way or some other debauchery that I do not condone. It amazes Me the lengths some go for satisfactions that are so despicable. It is as if a veil is over their eyes. The devil is a liar. He makes evil look good to those who are not mindful of the truth. My tools, for a life of satisfaction, are all in place. They are available for those who will just take the first few baby steps. I have My emissaries set to meet them at every crossroad if only they would stop, pray, and submit to My easy yoke. Then they would be set free. It is that simple. I weep at how they are so easily deceived following only the desires of the flesh thus denying their true feelings. They are neglecting the cry of their precious soul. These can only be saved through corporate prayer, fasting, and an intimate relationship with Me.

October 3

Opportunity for Change

The sins of the fathers and mothers revisit new generations despite heart knowledge of past destruction. It happens that the pattern cannot be broken easily. This follows the children into their precious lives and wreaks havoc in tragic ways. Be it alcohol, drugs, abuse, profanity, living an unchaste life, aggression, unforgiveness, jealousy, lies or thievery, all of these evils cling to many long after the innocence of childhood. Breaking the dreadful cycles can often take generations of heartache. As always, I am offering opportunities for change through life choices but, just as an addiction can seem impossible to break, these curses upon the spirit of man are powerful. So many are not aware of the spirit world of which I am a part. The enemy does indeed roam this earth looking for those he may devour. You would be shocked if you could see through spiritual eyes. That is why you must pray unceasingly for protection, guidance, wisdom, and grace to dwell on this earth. You must not succumb to the temptations of the devil. He is real and a threat to My creation. Believe this as with My Biblical promises. This is a truth that many just will not accept in faith. My Word is a sword that can battle these spirits. It is despicable to them. Do not be privy to deception and lies for they abound upon the earth. I give you free choice but you need My tools to survive.

October 4

Where are You?

And then there are those who accept Me and claim to be a Christian but I hardly know them. It is like a marriage in one sense, in that wonderful moment when they realize I am a reality bringing them those moments of bliss. Then after what I call the 'honeymoon period', they resume their lives. I am but a distant memory. Imagine getting married and having your spouse say "see you in a few weeks, years, or maybe never again." Yet still claiming outwardly to be married. There are those that think we should only be together in church or that is the only place I dwell. I can't be put in a box, any more than you can be. How can we get to know each other if you don't spend time with Me?

October 5

Listen for My Voice

As a potter can add clay to his creation, I am continually molding and shaping you to what I want you to be, but this can only be done through a willing heart. Then it is as if I now have the free will to lead you where you want to go anyway. Life will get visibly more exciting, My blessings more evident. As you hear My voice more clearly, I can better direct you to make good choices. Others around you will notice the change and be touched by you in a special way. It cannot be helped as inner beauty shines through. In My presence you would feel this as an all encompassing love radiating outward creating a palpable aura to those within reach. When you exude love, it bounces back. Try it.

October 6

Heed My Call

There is so much to be done. Poverty, sexual exploitation, abuse, hunger, thirst, despair, prostitution, depression, anger, hurt, resentment, family breakups, crime, and the list goes on of injustice and pain. You are My hands and feet. Heed My call to reach out daily even in small ways as the ripples can evolve into big breakers. Just a smile can brighten someone's day. Be ready to act, sometimes spontaneously, as you feel led by the Holy Spirit. A willing heart and spirit can go a long way in the earthly realm. If the act is good and lines up with My Word, fear not that you are carrying on My work.

October 7

Be as Willing to Receive as to Give

I have put those in your path to help guide you further in your walk. Even small daily happenings are not just random events. Those who are in need are abundant. A kind word or deed can set the mood for their day, sometimes for a lifetime. All of us have been touched by the kind acts of others. Be willing to receive as well as give. The blessings come on both ends.

October 8

Be Mindful of Beauty

Be watchful for the wonders around you. They are everywhere, often missed if not looked for in the busy whir of your day. The seasons change. With this the world and you are evolving. Marvel at even the smallest of miracles, the birth of a butterfly, the beauty of a luna moth, the bright orange glow of a harvest moon, rain drops clinging like crystals from the verdant greenery around you, the smell of balsum in the deep forest, the sound of birds, frogs, and crickets surrounding you. It is all for your enjoyment. Do not miss the pleasures I pour out to you daily by being too self absorbed.

October 9

Feel My Presence

Life moves along quickly especially as you grow in years. With it can come knowledge, wisdom, confidence, and, hopefully, a deeper spirituality. The world can rob you of some of these things due to stress, abuse, and other factors that can deplete inner resources. I can restore energy, vitality, hope, and beauty from the ashes of discouragement and pain. Reach out to Me in your darkest hour. I am here to rescue you. You will and have felt my presence.

October 10

The Truth Shall Set You Free

Knowing I am here for you should put a different dimension on your life .Where once alone and carrying all the burden, on shoulders bent with spirit broken, I come to restore, revive, and comfort. It is the acknowledgement of Me that brings your life's plan to fruition.

October 11

Allow the Holy Spirit

I long for all of My people to come to the understanding of My ways. Reading the Bible is one way to start, along with attending a Bible believing church run by Godly people who are not mired in the dogma that was so prevalent in My day. Believe Me, it still exists. My starving people search for Me and, instead, leave their places of worship empty. Why are so many fearful of the Holy Spirit, My gift, My promise to comfort and minister to a hurting world?

October 12

Love Thy Neighbor as Thyself

Reach out to all within your sphere. If others did the same we would have miniplanets of love and caring. Enough of these and how could strife continue? Instead My commandment to *love thy neighbor as thyself* would become a reality. How could war or famine exist in a world such as this?

October 13

Hope of Life Everlasting

With aging comes the loss of youth and loved ones. It also brings realization that life does not go on forever here on the earth. But the hope of life everlasting should sustain you. That is why it is so vital to press on even through the greatest of hardships. I am there to carry you on eagle's wings when necessary. Lean on Me for I am your strong tower, the rock or cornerstone of your foundation.

October 14

Seek My Face

I am your provider. My desire is to meet your needs physically, mentally, and spiritually. It is not for you to worry how all will come about. Seek My face and council. The answers will become evident if you are faithful to Me. You have seen others plans fulfilled. You are not alone. I have My hand upon your life. Be open to new challenges. They often lead you in a different direction, one I desire for you. Beware of self doubt. Have I not created perfect beings in My image? All are unique and hold special talents, even though not always visible. Search for Godly qualities in all you meet. You will be amazed to see them slowly unfold, like a rose bud opening to the sun. A simple smile can light up the world.

October 15

I Offer It to You

The wonders of this universe are there for all to behold. Look up at the star filled sky on a cloudless night. View the moon lighting up the darkness. You can be that light. Observe an infant as it explores its new world. Look, listen, smell, feel, and imbibe the pleasures of life. I offer all to you for the taking .Too many dwell on gloom and doom when the beauty of this life is tangible and within reach. It is as if the recipient of a gift refuses it or gives it back, much to the giver's dismay. Be of service to others if all else fails for in this you bring honor to yourself. Through your selfless acts you draw closer to Me.

October 16

Your Hand in Mine

I am sending those into your life who can help you achieve the desires of your heart. These desires often line up with My plan for you. You will feel the excitement if you have not already experienced it. That is how you know it is Me. Sleepless nights will allow you to become aware of some of what I have for you to do. Don't fret, for I will give you rest as you need it. Go forth in faith knowing I have your hand in Mine and Our best interests in mind.

October 17

Send Forth My Angels

The enemy will and has come against your loved ones as you draw closer to Me. My protection is over them but keep them in prayer. Place the full armor of God over each and every one of them daily. I send forth My mighty angels with a valiant alleluliah! We will do the rest.

October 18

My Hand is Upon You

Some days I put the name of someone I want you to minister to before you. You know who and what to do. Be assured that you will be a blessing to that person. You will build yourself up in faith through your actions. My best interests for you are always foremost. Go forth with the faith that I am leading you, My hand is upon you and yours. Your reward is at hand, My precious child.

October 19

I Have Made Provision

Be refreshed, even if just in the luxury of a hot shower. So many of My own lack this simple pleasure. Be thankful in even the little things. It starts there. Then look outward where you may be of service to others in small and large ways. I have made the provision, but so many of My people don't step forth. It is then in vain. The needs of this world are great. The urgency is now. I desire that you feel compelled. Act soon. Let Me show you how. I love that you are listening. Pass it on.

October 20

Oh, the Possibilities!

I wish to fill you with joy uncontainable. You can walk with Me here on earth long before you reach heaven. As you develop a closer relationship with Me, this intimacy brings greater responsibility. You can meet that challenge. I desire that bond with all of My people but, so many choose to ignore Me. Their loss is My loss as well. Choose a closer walk with Me and your life will burst open with possibilities.

October 21

I Long that the Veil be Lifted From Their Eyes

In this world of instant food, communication, and contact with others across the continents, the time is ripe to reach others for Me. It is urgent the veil over their eyes be lifted. My chosen people, originally the Jews, now to include the gentiles, still live in darkness when it comes to recognizing that ***I am the promised Messiah of the old testament!*** You can help, in your small way, to lift that veil. Boldly proclaim, in the name of Jesus, all that I have done and will do as written in the New Testiment. The Bible is indeed the chart in a world that needs direction. To consult its inspired words, written by so many of My saints, is not to be scoffed at. It has always been there to lead the way. It will forever be a best seller, while all other books will be forgotten.

October 22

Each Day My Gift to You

Enjoy this day, My gift to you, your day. Let it be a day in remembrance like no other day. Let it bring tears to your eyes to view the vibrant world around you. Know that you were created for My delight. It gives Me joy to dine with you and yours. Cherish Me first, then family, and lastly all of your brothers and sisters upon this earth with whom, I desire you to fellowship in peace. I know it is not true, as of yet, but each small contribution is like the starfish being thrown back in the ocean. It brings everyone a step closer to the perfect world I had hoped to create. Bask in the joy of this day as I wish for you many more to come. Put your hand in Mine. I will lead confidently the rest of the way on this eternal walk.

October 23

I Enfold You in My Peace

I will aid you in completing your work as needed in the days to come. By that I refer to mental, physical, and spiritual. The latter brings the greatest reward for, My voice must be heeded. When you are obedient, the angels rejoice. I draw you nearer. I long for this intimate connection with all who desire to know Me better. Your zest for learning more of Me, singing in adoration, and praying to Me to reveal your plan have never gone unnoticed. When you thought I was furthest away, I never left your side, even in the deepest of heartaches. The comfort you felt was Me enfolding you in My peace.

October 24

Lift Those up Who Need a Touch

Keep reaching out in new ways. Nursing homes, hospitals, prisons, and ghettos are among the places where there are those who need to be ministered to. Your heart should cry out in empathy for their trials. So many need an uplifting word. They also crave the companionship of others to bring them through yet another trying day. I never wanted them to end up this way, but through bad choices, unfortunate upbringing, and the influence of others they have been carried along often on a wave of evil, gathering others in their paths. Some are the unfortunate victims of poor physical health which brings its own pain, suffering, and despair. Be ready to acknowledge their, often silent, pleas to be noticed, helped, ministered to, and loved. Through their struggles, you will learn more of My mercy. My ability to use you to give hope and encouragement will bring you both nearer to My comforting presence.

October 25

Hang On

You continue to be surprised by what I am revealing. It just gets more exciting. Hang on. Enjoy the ride. The best is yet to come! I long to pour out My blessings on those who would accept them. If only they would realize that, by acknowledging Me, they start the flow of these blessings. The power of what can be done in My name is thrilling and sets hearts afire with a deeper love so amazing it's unexplainable. Imagine your first true love affair. It goes far beyond that. My love for you is so much deeper than you could ever fathom. I have loved you from thc beginning and will never leave you or forsake you. No one can make that promise. I stand by this and all of My Biblical promises as well. Trust in these to see you through the trials of life. My love is your covering

.

October 26

Serve Others

How can I be of service you ask? Just allow Me to guide you. If you truly want to fulfill My plan for you, you must be obedient, humble, bold, and willing. Some of these qualities seem to contradict the others but I've equipped you with what you need to go forth. Grasp, as a dying man does to his last breath, My garment in the form of service to others. For in this you gain the most ground for My cause. Each day ask Lord, what would you have me to do in Your name? I will answer you. Be still and listen for My voice.

October 27

Let Go

I have and will provide all you need in bringing you closer to your goals. Be it food, clothing, written material, or an expert in a certain field, I will give you the wisdom to know what to do or where to go with these things. I have made it simple, you are the one who wants to complicate matters with worry and confusion. Accept My gentle leading. Through this you will benefit the most. I have you in the palm of My hand. Let your worry, grief, sorrow, and resentments be placed there. Then let go of them never to take them back.

October 28

Temper Enthusiasm with Solemn Purpose

Temper your excitement and go forth with balance, fortitude, and a solemness knowing you are in a battle alongside Me. Keep silent when you yearn to burst over with the enthusiasm you are finding hard to contain. If you've not yet reached this point, you will if you are obedient, reverent, and heed My Words often found in the Bible. I'm giving you more of this enthusiasm to enhance your energy and sense of purpose. The quality of humbleness is one I treasure most. It is the haughty, so full of themselves with a false sense of power, that I find despicable. It was they who led the quest to crucify Me, placing on themselves, in the end, the greatest of remorse for what they had done. Their religious misdirection and dogma led them to the ultimate act of cruelty not knowing that, through it, I as well as all mankind, would be victorious.

October 29

Minister Always to Others

Go forth continuing to be of service to Me. Sometimes your 'job' is your disguise. The needs of this world are out there and must be met, but I give you the strength and energy to minister both in and out of that realm.

October 30

Despair Brings a Smile to Satan

Never give in to despair. Turn to Me in all things for I will sustain you through any storm and embrace you as you weather it. As a mother or father comforts a hurting child, I will be there for you. Never doubt this. My promises, laid out in My Word the Bible, have and will be fulfilled. Hang on to the truths of the Bible to sustain you. They will give you strength and wisdom to take the next steps in life.

October 31

Avoid the Trickery of the Devil

The spirit world is full of demons, ready to inhabit an unwilling soul. Beware of any trickery, masked in the form of fun, to lead you astray. The devil is an artful deceiver and takes many in his grasp without their knowledge. Beware of witchcraft, séances, ouija boards, fortunetellers, seers, wizards and others that portend to know the future. Unless Godly prophets sent by Me, known of the Holy Spirit, they are to be avoided at all costs. To become a victim to the Devil's wiles is not My plan for you but,with free will, you can place your foot in his trap. Seek My wisdom in these matters and what I have professed regarding them in My inspired Word.

November 1

Avoid the Idols of this World

Things are moving quickly in your world. Sometimes so fast that you can lose your grasp on reality and become a victim to it's grasp. The idols of daily living come and fade away, revered by many in blind pursuit of someone to follow other than Me. All is vain deception and to be avoided as a waste of purpose. It is another way the deceiver leads My people astray. Seek My face and I will set you on the right path.

November 2

You Must Not Give in to Grief

I give you tears to release the sorrow you hold inside. They are the thread I use to mend your heart. That is why it is important to let them flow as the urge arises. Tears of joy or worship are also vital to bring completion to the true emotion being felt. As the rain cleanses the earth, tears cleanse the body. Too many, as with any other excesses, can leave the body spent and the mind and spirit depressed. Tears are the opposite of laughter. Without them how could we compare the two emotions? To know the depths of happiness, we often must experience the depths of grief. Do not allow yourself to stay in the bottomless pit of grief for it will eat away at your spirit, making you numb to the many joys I still have in store for you.

November 3

Protect Yourself and Loved Ones

Speak to Me in prayer aloud, anoint yourself with oil, and cover yourself and loved ones with the full armor of God. Try to do this daily as it is a powerful link to Me and advised in My Word. Then you go out into a sinful world with added protection. Pray to do My will, for Me to send to you those who need your ministering touch, or who can bring you further on your journey. Seek to be a light to a world darkened by sins and oppression. This heaviness can often be felt in the air around certain circumstances or people. Be aware of this and pray for the lifting of this oppression in My holy name.

November 4

You are My Dinner Guest

Let your thoughts be of provision, not lack. I own the wealth of the universe and can parcel it out at My own whim. Do not tie My hands by speaking negatively or claiming poverty. You were created to partake of the feasts I lay before you. You are My dinner guest, to be served and to serve. The roles reverse themselves when necessary. Ask and it shall be granted with the stipulation that, if it is a Godly request and will fit the plan you are to be a part of, I will fulfill it at the proper appointed time. So many forget their requests and when I grant them, I hear not a word of thanks. If you but wrote your requests in prayer down, you would be amazed at how many have been answered. Then it would be a double blessing to you and Me as well.

November 5

Seasons of Your Life

Just as there are seasons in the world, there are seasons in your life. Changes are inevitable and through them you mature, learn, and become a better person if you seek to make Godly choices. This growth is immeasurable by you but if you could view it as your lifeline, you would be amazed at your journey. Those who have made wrong choices also can view and compare, make changes for the better, and continue the journey, not in a downward spiral but, hopefully up to Godly heights. I long to meet you there at the top of the mountain, victorious, the race well won. I am cheering you on. Be mindful of this and aim to please Me in thought and deed. I am smiling down on you with pleasure. Press on when life is difficult. This too will pass.

November 6

Your Work an Offering

Let your work on earth be done gladly with a cheerful heart and a thankful countenance. Try to please your heavenly father even with the most mundane of tasks. When you offer them as a sacrifice to Me, it is as fragrant incense wafting upward. I accept it and bless you for it.

November 7

Be Open to My Blessings

I long to pour out oceans of blessings on you and your loved ones. Be open to what I have in store for you. You will go forth with confidence then when trying to please Me. The joy that awaits you is uncontainable and will thrill you from head to toe. Sometimes you can feel the tingle of electricity go through you. You will know that it is Me. Bask in My love for I am happiest in your companionship.

November 8

Let Me Show My Care and Compassion

Just as you are beginning to realize, I am on time in so many of your life's struggles. Just when you think you cannot endure, or that a need will not be fulfilled, surprisingly I come through. This happens over and over again throughout life. Many do not take the time to thank Me, but, boy, did they ever complain when things weren't going their way! Others never seek My council even in the simplest matters but, if they did, I would show My care and compassion saving them so much needless frustration. Ask and it shall be given more often than not. Try Me. Allow My blessings to flow. It is that stubborn self reliance that is often man's downfall.

November 9

My Comfort is For All

I long to comfort those who are hurting. The pain in this world, in many forms, can be ministered to by you if you allow the Holy Spirit to open your eyes to it. You are beginning to empathize on a deeper level just through what you yourself have experienced. Don't you recall how often you've pleaded with Me to know why you've had to endure so much heartache? You are beginning to reap the fruit of your faithfulness, your courage to endure. I have comforted you so that you can know how to comfort others. The satisfaction you are experiencing is the feedback I desire for you to receive. The best is in the giving not the getting.

November 10

My Promise

Step out in courage knowing I am there to shore you up as needed. *I will never leave you or forsake you.* Those are powerful, potent words, My promise to you that My hand is upon you throughout this life and into the next. Just one of My promises I've given found in the Bible, the rest to be fulfilled if you remain faithful and obedient. Cling to these as lifelines to help you weather what has to come to pass and the storms of the future.

November 11

Take Your Hand Off the Rudder

Life's hardships strengthen your spirit to continue to endure. They enable you to empathize with the plight of others. The roller coaster of emotions you've traveled has brought you to where you are today. I say *enjoy the ride* for it can be a joyous one if you allow it to be. Let Me to be in control. Take your hand off the rudder. I will steer you to victory.

November 12

Be of Service to Others

There will be prophets, pastors, prayer warriors, intercessors, healers, deliverers from evil spirits, writers, singers, motivational speakers, radio, television, and computer to proclaim divine messages to a waiting world. Your are free to do your part, while discovering My plan for you. You are being of service to others. Be patient. All will fall into place.

November 13

Humble Yourself

Seek quiet secluded places of rest to restore your spirit and commune with Me. Do not forsake Me by neglecting My Holy Word or the fellowship of like believers. It is through these simple acts that your prayer and spiritual life will be strengthened to equip you for the daily tasks you must accomplish. Do all for Me, being a servant, for by humbling yourself your spirit rises up.

November 14

Service to Me is Freeing

Ripples of love radiate to others within their sphere. When they 'play it forward' a tidal wave of love can soften a stubborn heart. Why do they think that by serving Me they will become like prisoners? I strive to set the captives free from their oppression. It is the opposite of what they think will happen but fear and lack of wisdom often hold them back from tasting the fruit of redemption I offer in love.

November 15

Your Divine Assignment

I delight in you, My unique creation, fashioned in My image but with distinct qualities that distinguish you from all others. If your attributes are kept hidden, undiscovered, it becomes more difficult to fulfill your purpose and for Me to reveal your divine assignment. All have one, you know. It is just through listening to My voice in your quiet times communing with Me that I will reveal it.

November 16

I Will Equip You

My love for you is deep and enduring. As I gaze upon you daily My heart swells with love, admiration, and pride. You have traveled far on your journey. You have listened many times to My voice and followed the leading of your heart to perform deeds that have been pleasing to Me. Your sphere is widening. With it expect more responsibility. I will equip you to meet these greater challenges.

November 17

I Will Lead You

Consult My Word daily for direction and wisdom. Dwell in My presence. It takes only minutes, but brings lasting rewards. Divine inspiration can only take you further on your spiritual journey. Treasure its truths in your heart. Memorize verses to uplift and carry you through each day. It is by My leading that you will accomplish much in touching others with a heart for Me.

November 18

Cast Off Fear

Face each problem as a challenge to be met and conquered. Do not let fear enter into the equation. Always prayerfully seek My council first. It is when you look to the world for answers that you often stumble. In reaching out to Me I respond with love, grace, compassion, and a deep desire to fulfill your needs and wishes. Try Me.

November 19

As Servants You Become Royalty

I find despicable haughty arrogant scoffers so full of rebellion and pride. Satan chooses to abide with those of like mind. Seek power in the fear of the Lord by walking in humility when, as servants, you become royalty.

November 20

Fear Not Your Lord is Near

Just as I triumphed over death by crucifixion, you will be victorious soon enough in new glorified bodies. Yes, I ask, death where is thy sting? What do you have to fear when your precious Lord is near?

November 21

Continue in This Gift

And do not grieve the Holy Spirit of God by whom you were sealed for the day of redemption. (Ephesians 4:30)

The wind in all its power is not a match for the Holy Spirit. It has been known to change hearts and heal bodies. Do not fear speaking in tongues for that is one of the gifts which has been scoffed at. How else can you pray when, from the depths of your heart, you can't put into words your groanings? As long as you are not disruptive of other's worship continue in this God-given gift.

November 22

Touch Not My Little Ones

My children are as precious jewels more valuable than all the riches on earth. Let one hand be put upon them in harm and My wrath will be meted out. The injustices heaped upon these, unable to defend themselves, is unfathomable and an abomination in My name. Lo to those who participate in such debauchery for they are destined to the harshest punishment unless they repent of their ways, come to Me, and to their victims for forgiveness. I will not tolerate this despicable behavior as you were created in beauty to serve your loving God in acts of love and kindness. Children are to be protected, nurtured and loved. They are dearest to My heart.

November 23

I Am He to Which You Minister

It is when you minister to the sick, hungry, desolate, and abandoned that you are tending to Me. I am a part of all humanity as, in My image, we are all really as one. I may test you by bringing by one of these in need. By turning them away, when it is in your power to do more on their behalf, is a rebuke to Me. Prayer and sacrifice can do so much more than empty words. Search your heart in these instances and I will give you answers.

November 24

I **Will Come to Take You With Me**

I will come again to take you with Me to dwell in a paradise unequal to the Garden of Eden. Here is all you could ever ask or dream of in Godly companionship with the saints and those who have gone on before you. Your glorious reunion awaits along with a mansion suited just to you. Do not doubt this for these are My promises referred to in the Bible. I will fulfill them to your satisfaction.

November 25

My Plans Revealed

It is well you know not what lies ahead. Just as old age does not occur all at once, My plans are revealed gradually in amounts that you can digest. Much like a newborn unaccustomed to solid food you, as well, are not given more than you can handle before your time. In this way I gradually prepare you, in a sense, gently mold you like a ball of clay into your present state.

November 26

Exalt When Health is Good

Marvel at the wonders of the human body. Isn't it astonishing, it operates so efficiently, unnoticed by you as you go about your day? It is only when it shows pain or some other uncommon manifestation that you take notice. Exalt in your good health when it is apparent, for so many suffer daily in a myriad of ways. I am with them as well and help to quell their suffering Myself or through others I send. There are angels among you.

November 27

Taste of My Love

Too many fear Me which is unfortunate. Godly fear means to have a reverence and respect for Me. I would that My people who know Me would honor Me with praise, worship, and obedience . Our relationship can be a loving one if you desire that. It is My wish that this is what you would want for it is the desire of My heart. You could not fathom the depths of My love for you. All are precious in My sight worth more than the costliest treasures. Bask in My love for I show it to you daily in so many ways unnoticed by you.

November 28

Allow Me to be in Control

Worry not what you will wear, where you will live, or how you will spend your life in the future. I will guide you if you'll let Me. Were you to know the events of your life ahead of time, it would be too much to bear. The burden of what you face each day is enough for you to handle. If you would have Me first in your life, everything else would fall into place resulting in less frustration and increased joy. I repeat My promise, *My yoke is* easy *and burden light*. Come follow Me and a new life will open up to you.

November 29

Seek Me to Fulfill Your Goals

Not all will share your point of view, no matter how right you believe you are. All are at different levels of their walk, therefore they have not grown enough in some aspects of their lives to progress to the heights you have already reached. Sadly they may never attain this place in time if they are not seeking Me as their ultimate goal.

November 30

The Remarkable Human Body

The weariness of a day's work lets you know that you have done your part. Take mini breaks to refresh and replenish your energy supply. Tension and stress reside in a body that cannot stop, relax, and change gears. A brisk walk can clear the mind and loosen up a tense body. Know that the remarkable human body can bounce back from a negative place to a positive one with just a healthy diet, exercise, and spiritual breaks.

IN PRAISE OF HIM

December 1

Consume Me in Your Love

I long to be consumed in my worship of you, Lord. You are so faithful to us in your devotion, grace, and loving kindness. You are the only balm for a hurting world, the only answer to pain, sorrow, sickness, abuse, despair, and addiction. You are the healer of our afflictions. I will cling to the hem of your garment, for it is through drawing this near that I can be in your glorious presence.

December 2

You Dwell in Our Praises

I will forever praise you for it is in the praises of your people that you dwell. Yes, even if the rocks could cry out, the mountains sing, the trees converse they would, if they could, to show their devotion to you. I raise my arms as does the mighty tree heavenward to show my adoration. You have proven yourself to Me. In that I can forever breath easily. I know that you are my God and will glorify You for all my days.

December 3

Give it Away Be a Blessing

Material possessions are no longer of importance. You say give them away, I say gladly if it will brighten a life, or sooth a hurt. I know you look at us this way when you are bestowing your blessings upon us. Thank you for ever smiling down on us when we obey and listen to your heavenly voice. My heart sings as never before with the knowledge of your faithfulness and truths.

December 4

Reach Out and Take His Hand

I reach to take your hand as you extend it to me. I need your touch daily as the turmoils in today's world are getting too heavy for me to bear. Give me the strength to reach out to those, through you, to bring hope and light in the darkness. Carry me on eagle's wings forward in any of your assignments with a holy boldness in a more intimate walk with you. As my Creator I give you all the thanks and glory for all you have done, are doing and have yet to do in my lifetime.

December 5

Shout Alleluia the Victory is at Hand

In response to the above, it is indeed My pleasure to bestow My blessings on you and yours. In your faithfulness, the heeding of My voice, and your willingness to go forward, even when fear has been constantly on your doorstep, I say '***shout alleluia the victory is at hand***'. I and the angels rejoice at what is about to take place.

I long to pour out My blessings upon you and yours daily. Be expectant for you are dear to Me. I delight in you, the apple of My eye.

December 6

Storms of Your Life

Haven't I carried you through all the storms of your life as you look back upon them? I sent those who could minister to you as you needed it. Some in the form of angels others just the hands and feet of those like you. Your heart has always been turned toward Me, even in your doubt, you never quite let go or lost your sense of direction. Your desire to serve others is what draws them to you. Go forth as I give you My banner to lead the fight that must be fought. The victory will be won. My warriors will take charge when the time is ripe. Stand ready with the assurance that I am always with you in every battle just as I have been in the storms of your life.

December 7

Their Dying Like Mine the Ultimate Sacrifice

Father, if it is your will, take this cup [of suffering] away from me. however, your will must be done, not mine." Luke: 22:42

The death of one of My dear ones, at even a young age, can result in bringing others to Me, including family members. It may seem a harsh way to some but there are those that couldn't be drawn to Me in any other way. But, Oh the reward on the other side for that one who had to suffer in My name. Just as I had to make the ultimate sacrifice for My Father to complete His plan, these My special chosen ones, are sometimes the only answer to My saving grace. Do not despair as time is short. The reunion will be doubly sweet.

December 8

Forgive in Ernest

Then Peter came to Him and said, "Lord how often shall My brother sin against me, and I forgive him, up to seven times?" Jesus said to him, "I do not say to you, up to seven times, but up to seventy times seven." Matthew 18: 21-22

Matthew 18: 21-22

When you recall injustices in your life, it is so easy to relive that bitterness. The desire to strike out at that person or persons is palpable even now, perhaps years later. They must be forgiven as I forgave My persecutors. They really knew not the pain they were causing. You are reliving it by bringing it to remembrance. They are able to carry on life as usual. Who's suffering? Forgive, I say, and forgive again. Love conquers all hatred.

December 9

A Powerful Partner

Heaven awaits those who follow Me. You will marvel at its wonders. Do not fret that your loved ones are anything but happy there. Just as here, they all have assignments suited to their talents. Your pets await as well and will run, fly, crawl, hop, or swim to greet you. You cannot escape the love of the Lord. It is ever present. There are so many who are unaware of it and those suffer most. Depending on themselves or others to solve life's problems, there are many up against stone walls. If only they knew the true power of prayer, fellowship, the Word, but especially calling on Me, their lives would run so much more smoothly. Not to say there are not still trials and tribulations, it's just that with Me you have a powerful partner.

December 10

Be Still and Let Me Lead

My ways are unfathomable to man. The reasons for certain events in your life are best kept by Me for now. All will be revealed in eternity. Instead of trying to direct when you need to follow, be still and let Me do the work. I relish the chance to serve. Ask in complete faith. You will be impressed at what I can do for you for My storehouses are full. There is plenty in My land for all if you would share.

December 11

Take My Hand

I will take you forth in glory as you have obeyed Me having come humbly after Me in pursuit of wisdom and truth. Keep your hand within mine so that I may bless you as never before. I long to pour out blessings in abundance to My children, you who have sought My face so diligently. Accept and delight in My joy in you.

December 12

Seek the Holy Spirit

If you love Me, keep My commandments and I will pray the Father, and He will give you another Helper, that He may abide with you forever. John 14: 15-16

In this time of anticipation of the celebration of My birth, joy is palpable in the air. It could be this way all year long and should. This pleasure is available always, not just at Christmas time. It is there, through the Holy Spirit, in glad worship, or fervent prayer. I long to dwell in the presence of My people. This happens so easily in praise, but so many churches need teachings in the art of praise. To most it comes naturally, but inhibitions hamper its expression. Seek to learn at a church that exhibits this uninhibited praise. It is available for viewing to some through television. Notice the apparent joy and gladness, never mind the tangible presence of the Holy Spirit in that atmosphere of heartfelt pleasure. I can lead you to such a church where you can learn of the delight you can experience daily through worship, praise, prayer, and adoration. Just ask and I will show you. Be not afraid to experience this gladness of heart and soul. It is My greatest wish for you and a part of My plan for your fellowship with Me. Why else would I create you but for you to fellowship with Me in such a joyous way until we can be together in eternity? This uplifting, felt through joint adoration, prayer, and praise, is My plan for worship here on earth. It is one of the greatest gifts you can experience, rivaling any material gift you could receive. Religious dogma, indifference, and ritual has driven this out of My churches leaving much dissatisfaction among those seeking My face. Search for the Holy Spirit, other than salvation, the greatest of My gifts here on earth in a church where it is acknowledged not avoided. It was My promise for the world following My resurrection. Why do churches ignore this, the greatest of My gifts, left by Me for My people until My return? It is indeed the comforter I promised to be sought by all with diligence. I freely give it to those who seek and desire it.

Salvation and the Holy Spirit are available to all, just ask and they are yours.

December 13

I Will Meet Your Every Need

Trust in Me to provide for your needs. Do not let insecurity rule your life for, if you seek Me in prayer, I will meet you where you are. I often know of what you are in need before you do. Haven't I been there before for you? Put your faith in Me to continue providing what you lack. It is My pleasure to show you what I can do. I will guide you and put those in your path who can provide a way. Seek Me in prayer when you are uncertain of the direction you should go.

December 14

Never Claim Illness

To rid yourself or another of afflictions you can bind that spirit that is not of Me. The way to do it is to say this prayer or one similar: *Oh Lord bind that spirit that is not of you, but of the devil and bring it to the deepest depths of hell from whence it cannot return.* I will honor such a prayer and release that person of the stronghold of which he is in possession. Never say " I bind" with the word *devil* or *Satan* even close to it (pronoun I). You never want the devil anywhere near yourself, especially in a spoken sentence. Remember your words are powerful. Didn't My Father cause the world into existence with words? That is why your negative words of discontent, prediction, or acceptance of illness (*I have*) can wreak such havoc with your mind, spirit, or body. Never say "I have (cancer, anxiety, depression, arthritis, etc.) as you are claiming that it is indeed in possession of you. You could say " I

battle with what ever ailment it is, but I am believing for healing."
Heed these warnings for they are My truths.

December 15

Face and Conquer Evil With Holy Boldness

Love one another as I have loved you. There is no room for hate, discontent, envy, strife, unfaithfulness, lies, thievery, debauchery, or any other evil under the sun in My perfect world. Yet you allow it by not speaking out to these injustices. Be bold to rid humanity of evil. To remain silent when the wrongs of this planet are evident is to be living a lie. Be bold in ridding My perfect world of its imperfections. For this I will smile down upon My faithful warriors who do battle with evil and ultimately win. For I am on their side in this battle to bring it to an end, in My name. Go forth with My holy boldness knowing you are to be victorious.

December 16

My Songs Stir Your Heart

Listen often to My songs of praise written by the dear, inspired artists who created them. They will minister to your spirit. Sing out to Me as well for I hear the praises of My people in word, action, and song. You will be blessed, your spirit will be ministered to, and you will feel My presence near more often than not. For what would the world be without music to shore up your spirits when feeling down, tired, or hopeless? I give you instruments to bring forth a variety in sound. Your voices combined with these reach Me as a sweet incense. Strive to put more music in your lives and a song will abide in your heart when you most need it.

December 17

Restore Your World

I weep for the destruction of My world through pollution, clear cutting, poor land use, and all out neglect. Nurture what I've provided and all can benefit. Continue as you have and your supply is no longer seemingly endless. I give wisdom to see what has and will happen. It is for those bold ones to go forth and reclaim My world. Bring it back to its original beauty. It can be done and must be before there is no turning back.

December 18

I Embrace You in the Storm

You are being constantly amazed at what I am doing in your life. Each step has been ordered. Those who need you are within reach of you. All is going forth as I hoped and planned because you have fought the fear that torments you. You have been bold in your walk with Me. Continue and so many will be blessed. You will be through them. You are being swept along as in a tornado but the aftermath is one of joy and restoration rather then death and destruction. Enjoy My presence for I embrace you in the storms of life.

December 19

Go Forth in Obedience

You are nearing the end of one journey but will begin another soon. This one will be even more to your liking, I promise you.

Life is ever changing, sometimes for the good other times not. Each turn is molding you to what you need to be. Just go forward with the thought to please Me and be obedient. All else will be put into your hands at the proper time. Be faithful and trust in Me. Marvel at My grace and loving kindness.

December 20

Think of Your Gift Unacknowledged

As I have said, My time is not your time. Often prayer requests do not get immediately granted. That is why many forget what they have even prayed. When prayer is answered, though grateful for the outcome, the recipients often forget to thank Me. Acknowledgement of Me and all I have done, am doing, and will do, brings you that much closer to Me. Did you know we often sing together, although My voice is in the spirit in accompaniment. Then your immersion in that spiritual moment is palpable. That is the fulfillment you feel in the spirit when your voice joins Mine in joyous reverie. My divine assignment, paid in full, was to come to earth and live as you do. I walked in persecution, suffering indignity so that I could know the joys and sorrows of life in the flesh. I communed with the apostles and continue to dine with you. If it is what you desire, your walk with Me can bring the ultimate delight and pleasure. Choose Me over the world's temptations in the flesh. You will never regret it. Wait expectantly for your next 'divine assignment' for they continue if you listen expectantly to My voice. I find great pleasure in your devotion to Me, extending My hand to continue our walk, My precious child.

December 21

Heed the Silent Cries of the Downhearted

During this joyous time seek those who suffer, even more diligently. The happiness others are experiencing makes the plight of the downhearted all the more evident and painful. Be attuned to the atmosphere that surrounds those I put you together with. Your empathy will extend out to them, allowing you to minister mightily if you but follow My gentle leading. You can be a light in the darkness changing despair to hopeful joy in the matter of an instant with your touch, words, or a heartfelt prayer. Move forward in faith allowing the Holy Spirit to powerfully intervene. Changing lives, one at a time in My name, is My goal for you. The challenges you've already met assure Me that you are up to the task. My love continues to surround you, shoring you up on eagle's wings to greater heights. Fly with Me. Together we make an unbeatable team!

December 22

Well Done My Faithful Servant

I long to say to you "*Well done My faithful servant.*" and to place a crown of glory upon your head. Your name is known on earth and in heaven in My book of life. Acknowledge all I say to you in the course of a day, desiring to fulfill My will for your life. I never said it would be easy, but I did promise to give you life and more abundantly. Partake of My blessings for I heap them upon you as you go forth in obedience. Victory is ours, My beloved.

December 23

Carry Forth the Banner

This is your chance to minister to a hurting world. Proceed with others of like mind to carry the banner of hope, light, and fulfillment through Me. I provide all that is needed in My Holy Spirit, your advisor and comforter. Go forth boldly never allowing fear to gain a foothold in the perfect life I've fashioned for you.

December 24

The Night I Was Born

On the night that I was born the angels rejoiced in heaven along with My Father and those on earth who heeded the predictions of the prophets. That light filled appointed night new life, attainable to all, came in the form of an innocent baby. My mother knew not of the heartache I would cause her before it was finished. To partake briefly of your earthly life gave Me insight into your struggles. Through the experience I became close to mankind in a new way. As you are going through struggles think of Mine. What I endured to purchase you for My father's kingdom you cannot even imagine. Your struggles will not seem as insurmountable in comparison.

December 25

The Supreme Gift

Today many, but not all, are celebrating the day of My birth. Sadly there are those to whom My name does not even come up in their thoughts or conversation. To them it is about the material of this earth, the gifts, when My supreme gift is ignored. They've been taught, shown, ministered to but they remain blind to Me. Yet there is still time for them. Through a book such as this or perhaps someone who can penetrate the barrier of their hardened heart will they be introduced to Me, their Creator. I wait patiently to rejoice with the angels when another of My dear ones awakens to the reality of it all. Never pass up a chance to minister to one of these, My lost sheep who have gone astray.

December 26

My Love Flows Down From Heaven

The love I have for those of this world is uncontainable. It flows down from heaven in a steady stream, softening hearts to be receptive to My Word either in print or spoken by my elect. I long to sooth the world's ills with its healing balm. Through you and others like you, who can become My hands and feet, they will be drawn in by the multitudes to My delight. I await as a loving father with open arms and a joyful heart. I desire the best for My beloved children. I long to draw them to My heart to heal, comfort them, and renew their spirits. I will assure them of My authority with a touch from the Holy Spirit, My promised comforter ever ready to minister to My people. He is gentle and seeks permission before going forth into a heart that truly desires His presence.

December 27

Embark on an Exciting Journey with Me

This year is ending but a new one is soon to start. Many will view it as a fresh beginning. There are those who will embark on their journey with Me. That is very exciting for them as Me. Others will go on blindly pursuing money, power, knowledge of this earthly world, and objects that will tarnish and fade away. So many will continue to be captives of sin and its ensnarement, disillusioned following the often chosen path. All need prayer, protection, human intervention, and knowledge of Me as their savior, redeemer, and Lord. If only they knew that by the simple act of acknowledging Me, their shackles would be broken, they would be set free to find the joy that has been alluding them. As always *I will never leave them or forsake them.* It is they who need to find their way back to Me.

December 28

My Prodigal Sons and Daughters

I, as their Father, wait for their return. Just as the story in the Bible relates the joy of the father whose prodigal son has been away so long, I await with open arms no matter what they have done or how they have sinned. My grace is sufficient to cover all transgressions. I will cast their sins and iniquity into the depths of hell never to be thought of again by Me. With My help they can let it go too. Then I and all the angels of heaven will rejoice that a son or daughter has returned to the fold.

December 29

Join in Corporate Prayer

As the New Year approaches, all should join in prayer in their respective churches, synogogues, or dwellings if unable to get out and fellowship with others. Their prayers should center around world peace, protection for another year from the evil one, and most of all that My people will return to be a nation with a strong faith and commitment to Me.

So much good could be accomplished in unity of purpose to end world wide hunger, poverty, pollution, sickness, sin, and ignorance. Corporate prayer is powerful, beckoning the Holy Spirit within its midst. Continue to anoint each other with oil and minister to each others needs. The time is short until My return. Be ready. The signs of the prophets are being fulfilled. Be mindful of this. Be vigilant in your desires to know more of Me and what I would have you to do.

IN PRAISE OF HIM

December 30

You Are An Awesome God

How can you measure the love and mercy of God? It is beyond comprehension. As He has ministered to you and me through this book, a work has been done already. Even before we go out into the world, He has ministered to us through his loving kindness in the words he has imparted to our souls and spirits through his Holy Spirit. As you and I go out, let us acknowledge the solemn responsibility upon each one of us to reach the lost for Him. We are already equipped with the tools we need which include the Holy Bible, a Bible believing church open to the urgings of the Holy Spirit free of dogma (if not seek one), the ability to set aside time to commune with Him in prayer to seek His face, and the saving relationship found only through acceptance of the Lord as your savior. If you are lacking any of these, you are not equipped for battle. Do not delay in fulfilling the requirements to be a servant for Him. You will never regret it for, the rewards of this world are temporal. Heaven awaits His faithful.

December 31

Bring With You the Lost

As the New Year approaches, I put before you a fresh adventure. Old things have passed away. You have the chance to go forth with a glad heart, freed of any heaviness. My grace is sufficient to carry you to new heights if you but step in closer to Me for a fresh anointing. It is not far. Time is short. Together we can conquer even the toughest of challenges. I AWAIT YOU AT THE BRIDGE TO ETERNITY. My wish is for you to take with you as many as are lost, filled with new hope and a desire for A Closer Walk.

For all have sinned and fall short of the glory of God being justified freely by His grace through the redemption that is in Christ Jesus. Romans 3:23

If you confess with your mouth the Lord Jesus and believe in your heart that God has raised Him from the dead, you will be saved. Romans 10: 9-10

A Version of the Sinner's Prayer

Precious heavenly Father, I know I have sinned and fallen short of the hope You have for Me
I ask you to cleanse my heart of all sin and unrightiousness
You made the ultimate sacrifice by crucifixion so that not one of us is lost to the ravages of sin in a wicked world
Accept my humble pleadings to free me of the bondage of sin and forgive me for any wrong doing that is unpleasing to You
I come to You empty handed but full of hope for a new life through an intimate relationship with You
Accept my prayer so that I may become a child of God to the rejoicing of You and Your angels today in Heaven
Amen

(Author's Note)
It is only through grace that we become children of God. The acronym Grace translates into **G**od's **R**ighteousness **A**t **C**hrist's **E**xpense.

PEACE BE WITH YOU

Acknowledgements

I'd like to thank my God who guided me in the writing of this book from its inception to completion. Next, let me thank my husband Maury who has been ever supportive and encouraging often putting up with my writing late into the night. I'd also like to thank my church family for their support during the trials and triumphs of this year long 'divine assignment.' I'd especially like to thank the late Robert Noyes, my beloved pastor for many years, so Christ like in his love for others and his wife Janice who agreed to edit this book. She has been invaluable in keeping its writings scriptural and in line with the Bible's teachings. Next I am so proud to acknowledge my current pastor, The Reverend Tammy Noyes and her husband Robert, the son of Robert and Janice, for their dedication in carrying out the Lord's work. They and their small congregation, when faced with the challenge of starting a new church, proved that by trusting in a loving God, He would provide. The current church, The Carmel Full Gospel Church of Restoration in Carmel, Maine is a testament to God's faithfulness and the endurance of those who believed that **all things are possible** for those who put their trust in God and his promises. Others who have been an encouragement in directing my path to this book's publication include my family, Vicki Schad, Edie Cunningham, Genie Daley, Cheryl Mckeary, Judy Hardy, Kelly Hewins, Frank Harding, and Hannah Shively. Special thanks to Travis Russell for setting up my website www.gloriapowell.com. My son Matthew Thibodeau was integral in helping with the technical assistance in uploading this book in Kindle format. Lastly, I'd like to thank my grandparents who have gone on to be with the Lord, Hazel and Ernest Boulay, for instilling in me a love of God that has helped sustain me through life's trials and enabled me to create this book.

G.J.P.

Made in the USA
Middletown, DE
23 November 2021

52705240R10106